STEWARDS OF THE STORY

STEWARDS OF THE STORY

STORY

The Task of Preaching

James Earl Massey

WESTMINSTER
JOHN KNOX PRESS
LOUISVILLE · KENTUCKY

Scripture quotations, unless otherwise indicated, are from the New Revised Standard Version of the Bible, copyright © 1989 by the Division of Christian Education of the National Council of the Churches of Christ in the U.S.A., and used by permission.

Scripture quotations marked TNIV are from *Today's New International Version.* Copyright © 2001, 2005 International Bible Society. Used by permission of Zondervan Bible Publishers.

Excerpt from "We Will Work for Jesus," by Daniel S. Warner, no. 520 in *Worship the Lord,* copyright © 1989 by Warner Press, Inc. Used by permission of Church of God Ministries, Inc.

Excerpt from "Andrew," by Clive Sansom in *The Witnesses,* copyright © 1956 by Eyre Methuen. Used by permission of David Higham Associates.

Book design by Sharon Adams
Cover design by Night & Day Design

First edition
Published by Westminster John Knox Press
Louisville, Kentucky

This book is printed on acid-free paper that meets the American National Standards Institute Z39.48 standard. ♾

PRINTED IN THE UNITED STATES OF AMERICA

06 07 08 09 10 11 12 13 14 15—10 9 8 7 6 5 4 3 2 1

Library of Congress Cataloging-in-Publication Data is on file at the Library of Congress, Washington, D.C.

ISBN-13: 978-0-664-22981-8
ISBN-10: 0-664-22981-6

To
Dean Timothy George
and
the Faculty, Staff, and Students
at
Beeson Divinity School,
beloved colleagues
in the ministry of the gospel

Contents

Foreword by Timothy George	ix
Preface	xv
1 The Preacher as God's Steward	1
2 The Steward as Recitalist	11
3 The Steward and Rhetoric	25
4 The Steward and Ritual	35
5 The Steward and Reality	41
6 The Gracious Imperative: A Sermon	51
7 On Being a Leader: A Sermon	59
8 This Jesus: A Sermon	67
9 On Being Responsible: A Sermon	73
10 Stay in the Race! A Sermon	77
11 When Devotion Meets Difficulty: An Easter Sermon	85
Notes	93
Index of Names	103
Index of Biblical References	107

Foreword

I first heard the voice of James Earl Massey when I was a theological student at Harvard Divinity School and he was the stated preacher for the Christian Brotherhood Hour, a weekly international broadcast sponsored by the Church of God (Anderson, Indiana). In those days, homiletics was not a regular part of the curriculum at Harvard. As a young minister with a small pastoral charge, I was eager to learn all I could about the craft of preaching, especially in a multiracial, inner-city congregation. James Earl Massey was different from any other radio preacher I had ever heard. His diction was perfect, his command of the English language superb, his style lively and compelling, though never marked by ostentation. He also had a way of getting on the inside of a biblical text, of unraveling it, so to speak, not like a botanist studying a leaf in a laboratory, but like a great singer offering a distinctive rendition of a famous song.

Music is an apt analogy for Massey's preaching. Early on he received advanced training in classical piano and had all the makings to become a refined concert artist. The modalities of music—rhythm, pitch, tone, phrasing, cadence, melody, mood—also apply to the work of the preacher, and Massey is a master of them all. When his career path turned from music to the ministry, the world lost a great pianist but gained a magnificent preacher of the gospel. For Massey, though, preaching is never a mere performance, however well honed and powerfully presented. The sermon is more a deliverance than a performance: what is said is more important than how we say it, though these two aspects can never be completely divorced.

In any event, Massey was propelled into his life's work by a palpable sense of divine calling. As a young man of sixteen, he had come to the sanctuary of the Church of God in Detroit one Sunday morning with the score of a waltz by Chopin in his hands, intending no doubt to work on his musical assignment if the sermon proved boring! Here is how he describes what happened: "But during a brief let-up in my concentration on the score, I found myself being captured by the spirit of the worship occasion. As I honored the meaning of the worship hour and opened myself to God, I felt caught up into an almost transfixed state, and I heard a Voice speaking within my consciousness: 'I want you to preach!'" In that "great listening moment of grace," the trajectory of Massey's life was redirected. As he puts it, "the Voice that called me was so clear and its bidding, though gentle, bore the unmistakable authority of a higher realm." Five years later, in 1951, he was ordained to the Christian ministry.

Across the years, James Earl Massey has poured his life into the service of the church in numerous ways that have touched the lives of thousands of others. As the apostle Paul wrote to the Corinthians, so Massey too could say to many whose lives and ministries have been decisively shaped by him: "You yourselves are our letter, written on our hearts, known and read by everyone. You show that you are a letter from Christ, the result of our ministry" (2 Cor. 3:2–3 TNIV). He has been a pastor, scholar, teacher, evangelist, theological educator, denominational counselor, and respected leader in the world Christian movement. These are all positions—influential positions—he has held in fulfillment of that prior calling he received one Sunday morning in 1946 at a worship service in Detroit. In each of these roles, the task of preaching has been central. The desire to do pulpit work well, to the glory of God and for the blessing of all who hear, has ever claimed the deepest passion of James Earl Massey.

Massey is the heir of a rich heritage of faith. Brought up in a home marked by warmhearted Christian devotion, Massey was spiritually formed by Wesleyan theology, the Holiness movement, and the African American tradition. The rich spiritual resources of these cultural and church traditions have always informed, and are still reflected in, Massey's approach to ministry and preaching. But there is a sense in which he transcends them all. The quest for authentic Christian unity is a major motif that runs deep through all of Massey's work. Whether the issue is racial segregation, gender discrimination, or denominational fragmentation, Massey has emphasized the gospel's call to ecclesial unity and spiritual equality based on the new reality that has come into being through the community of Jesus Christ and the outpouring of the Holy Spirit. In this, and in other respects as well, he has followed in the footsteps of the great Howard Thurman, one of his mentors and special friends.

Much of the material in this book was presented as the William E. Conger Jr. Lectures on Biblical Preaching at Beeson Divinity School in February 2004. Dr. Massey has spoken many times at our school, and his messages have always been substantive, insightful, and inspiring. But his lectures on "Stewards of the Story," representing, as they do, "vintage Massey," had a special effect on our community. Here we have the mature analysis of a master preacher reflecting on the meaning of his craft and exhorting the rising generation of men and women— those who have been called by the same Voice that summoned him— to be faithful to the deepest impulse of their vocation. There is wisdom in this book for pastors and preachers everywhere, as well as for all those who listen to them, but there is an undercurrent of urgency that applies directly to the preachers of tomorrow.

The burden of this book runs counter to much that is thought and said about preaching today. In Massey's depiction of "The Story," the definite article makes a particular point. Preaching is not merely about *stories*, understood as a disparate collection of personal experiences, memories, recollections, and intuitions divorced from the narrative unity of the Bible read as a whole. The fragmentation and disconnection of much contemporary preaching is a reaction, or perhaps an over-reaction, to certain totalizing and oppressive ways the Christian Story has sometimes been told in the past. Postmodernist thinkers offer a helpful critique to such domineering uses of the biblical text, and we need to hear what they have to say. But Massey is right to call us back to a fresh encounter with the canonical shape of biblical revelation. The Story is good news: good news about what God has once and for all done in the history of redemption, and once and for all said in the Bible. The undeniable diversity found in the Scriptures does not obscure the fact that we are dealing here with one *biblion*: a coherent account of God's purpose for the world and for each of us.

God-called preachers, Massey argues, are *stewards* of this amazing Story. There is great joy in such a stewardship, but it brings a burden as well. Story-stewardship implies a unique calling, a divine commissioning, a holy accountability, and a distinctive demeanor among those who would handle it well. Stewards of the Story are not just like everyone else, only more so! Although most Protestants do not regard ordination as the impartation of an indelible quality on those set apart for the church's service in this way, there is nonetheless a special responsibility, a certain shaping of character, that comes from being entrusted with such a stewardship. The New Testament describes the message of salvation in Christ as something "sure and worthy of full acceptance" (1 Tim. 1:15 RSV). The truth of the message is not tied to the fidelity of the messenger, but its credibility in the world certainly is. "Love one another," said Jesus. "By this everyone will know . . ." And again, "Let your light shine before others, that they may see . . ." (John 13:34–35; Matt. 5:16 TNIV).

Recital, Massey says, is at the heart of the steward's work, and this requires careful attention to rhetoric. "Rescue a word . . . discover a universe," the famous Cambridge New Testament scholar Edwyn C. Hoskyns once said to his hearers. "Can we bury ourselves in the lexicon," he asked, "and arise in the presence of God?" The Christian Story is about words as well as the Word. Those who take seriously their charge to proclaim God's life-giving word of judgment and grace will not succumb to sloppiness in speech, extemporaneous fluff, or a pedestrian banality that can neither rise to majestic heights nor stoop to lend a sympathetic ear. In a culture that values images more than words, Massey asks us to pay attention to the way we tell the Story, to the linguistic forms through which our ideas are conveyed, and, beyond this, to the art of reading the Bible, to learning all over again the central story line of the New Testament: "In the past God spoke . . . through the prophets . . . but in these last days he has spoken to us by his Son" (Heb. 1:1–2 TNIV).

Recital requires rhetoric, and it is also best done with ritual. Ritual can degenerate, of course, into mere ceremony, or, even worse, become a pretext for an inordinate focus on the external details of order and office. When ritual becomes ritualism in the preacher's work, then the authenticity of our message is in jeopardy. "Nothing is so deadening to the divine," George MacDonald wrote, "as an habitual dealing with the outsides of holy things." For Massey, though, ritual is always in the service of the message, never a substitute for it. "Every sermon we deliver," Massey says, "ought to report what God has sent us to say on his behalf." True preaching is not clever words strung together in an entertaining manner "to charm away an hour or two of dull Sabbaths," as one nineteenth-century observer characterized certain popular clerics of his day. Rather, we need pastors who preach because they, like Jeremiah, have a fire in their bones—heralds of the gospel who, like Paul, are compelled by the love of Christ.

The unifying center of the preaching moment remains the fidelity and clarity of the message on the one hand, and the passion and integrity of the messenger on the other. Stewards of the Story are preachers who speak the truth in love "dipping and seasoning all our words and sentences in our hearts before they come into our mouths . . . so that our auditors may plainly perceive that every word is heart-deep" (George Herbert).

Stewards are trustees, into whose care and responsibility something precious—in this case, something infinitely precious—has been entrusted. In the most basic sense, trustees are not "owners" of the prized bequest they have received. Rather, they hold the bequest in trust, and they have a fiduciary responsibility to pass it on intact to those who will one day receive it in turn from them. Preachers of the gospel are trustees of the Story. To discharge this duty faithfully requires not only a knowledge of the Story's content, but also the kind of wisdom that comes only through the hard work of listening, praying, serving, loving, and representing the One in whose name we speak and for whose sake we do this work.

I once heard the work of the preacher compared to that of a mail carrier—someone charged to deliver a message, a message written by someone else, a message of great urgency addressed to every single person in the world. In an age before e-mails and faxes, it was all the more important that "the mail get through," even if this required those who carried the letters to go through rain, hail, snow, inhospitable terrain, and even enemy territory to make the delivery. Yes, preachers are like such devoted persons of the post, but with this difference: the message we carry to others is addressed to us as well. We who are stewards are also claimed by the Story's demands and promises. We deliver to others that which we have also received.

Never one to give himself to minor absolutes, James Earl Massey has modeled, with courage and compassion, the burdensome joy of a herald whose life reflects the message he proclaims. For more than half a century, Dr. Massey has been a faithful steward of the Story. He is a worthy guide for those whom the Master has called and sent forth to preach.

TIMOTHY GEORGE

Preface

Some justification for this book might seem demanded, since it is my fifth treatment in print regarding the preacher's calling and task.[1] The present study differs from the previous ones in both focus and detail.

This book treats four factors that influence the Christian sermon: the recital cast of the biblical narratives; the rhetorical demand for recasting the biblical message for our own time; the ritual setting in which preaching takes place, and how that setting affects the atmosphere and activity of the preaching deed; and the realities that inform us for preaching—the human realities to which we must give attention and the divine realities to which we point in witness as "good and faithful" stewards.

And now a word about the title. Readers of my earlier books about preaching will have seen frequent references made to "The Story."[2] This expression is from the Black Church tradition and it gathers up all that we see in the biblical message, but with special focus on the life and ministry of Jesus. In our way of speaking, The Story immediately recalls one or more of the three levels to which African American believers are sensitive in our contact with Scripture: (1) the events reported there as happenings; (2) the canonical interpretation of those events; and (3) the divine action associated with the reported happenings.[3] Christian preaching has to do with telling The Story, and doing so with a sense of history, a settled faith-perspective, and an acquaintance with God who is at work in human history. The Christian preacher is a steward of The Story, a person entrusted to administer biblical truth as a steward of the God and Father of Jesus Christ, an agent intent and eager to see the consequences of that telling effected in personal and social history. Thus this book and its title.

This book is an expanded version of the twelfth annual William E. Conger Jr. Lectures on Biblical Preaching, which I delivered at Beeson Divinity School, Samford University, Birmingham, Alabama, in February 2004. Some additional convocation and chapel addresses I delivered there and at Howard University's Rankin Chapel are also included. The invitation from Dean Timothy George to give the 2004 lectures made me feel especially privileged in that it allowed me a "second time around" experience, after being the Conger lecturer previously in the spring of 1995. I am indebted to Dean George and to President Thomas E. Corts for their many kindnesses. An accepted assignment was again not only an occasion of honor but a delightful service role. In an earlier version, chapters 2 through 5 were delivered during the spring of 2000 at the McAfee School of Theology of Mercer University, in Atlanta, Georgia, as the William L. Self Lectures on Preaching. Dean R. Alan Culpepper, an esteemed scholar and longtime friend, honored me through his invitation. It was particularly a joy for me to join in honoring Dr. Self, the lectureship honoree, with whom I had shared pulpit responsibilities several times across the years during national conferences on preaching.

Portions of chapter 1 were first used as a plenary address in Dallas, Texas, during the 2002 E. K. Bailey International Conference on Expository Preaching, and again at Phillips School of Theology, in Atlanta, Georgia, in January 2004 during the seminary's eighth annual pastors' conference.

JAMES EARL MASSEY

1

The Preacher as God's Steward

One of the most incisive, instructive, engaging, and humbling biblical images of the Christian preacher is that of "steward." There are several biblical references to persons who were stewards, and an exploration of those settings would help to highlight the importance of the image that is before us; but perhaps a definition of the word "steward" will suffice as we begin, and then a consideration of some New Testament texts in which preachers are addressed as such, together with a statement of their implications for ourselves and our work.

I

As for definition, the New Testament uses the word "steward" with reference to someone who oversees, administers, manages, under a commissioning trust that authorizes them to do so. The most common New Testament Greek term for "steward" is *oikonomos*, the background of which has to do with managing family (*oikia*) or household (*oikos*) matters. The steward held a trusted appointment to manage something in the interest of the one who owned it. The scope of that trust is readily sensed as one reads the Old Testament references to Eliezer, Abraham's steward (Gen. 15:2; chap. 24), and to Joseph's steward (Gen. 43:19–24; 44:1–6), or the New Testament references in several of the parables of Jesus (i.e., Matt. 20:8–9; Luke 16:1–8) that mention the responsibilities, privileges, problems, resourcefulness, and deeds of stewards.[1]

As for texts, it was the apostle Paul who applied the image of steward metaphorically to the work of the preacher, in two conspicuous places:

1 Corinthians 4:1–2	Think of us in this way, as servants of Christ and stewards of God's mysteries. Moreover, it is required of stewards that they be found trustworthy.
Titus 1:7	For a bishop, as God's steward, must be blameless; he must not be arrogant or quick-tempered or addicted to wine or violent or greedy for gain.

The apostle Peter extended the application of the stewardship image to inform all believers that they are entrusted persons. Thus 1 Peter 4:10, with this instruction to all Christians: "Like good stewards of the manifold grace of God, serve one another with whatever gift each of you has received."

In keeping with the theme of this gathering, it is important to think of our stewardship in relation to the tasks, concerns, and issues of ministry, and to do that thinking guided by the theological method of the Wesleyan Quadrilateral, with Scripture, tradition, reason, and experience as our guiding norms.[2] Scripture is foundational for understanding our task; tradition informs us about how ministry has been done and passed on to us; reason helps us to understand, explain, and systemize our task; and experience has to do with how we embrace and make that task our very own, intent to be faithful as stewards of it all.

I hardly need to remind the reader of the strategic timeliness of our focus on the importance of these four guiding norms: Scripture is under attack in our time as provincial, partial, and nonapplicable—even in some conventional churches. Tradition is viewed by many as too binding, and there is a growing revolt to be independent from the past, to break with what has been valued, thought, said, and done by sainted believers in all earlier times and movements before this one. As for the norm of reason, and the norm of experience, the arrogant intellectualism and consumerism in our culture have made idols of self-thought and self-will, so that nothing is reasonable or worthy of being experienced except what one prefers for oneself. Given this time and setting in which we serve, the importance of our task bids us to think carefully, intentionally, and prayerfully about our task, so that our understanding, our attitudes, our actions, and our expectations will be in line with what God desires, has planned, and requires on our part as commissioned stewards.

II

You will have noticed that in the 1 Corinthians 4:1 text Paul described the province of the preacher's stewardship as handling and heralding "the mysteries of God."

In Pauline usage "mystery" (*mysterion*) has to do with the historical action of God, with how God enacted and enacts his salvific purpose in this world. Mystery encompasses that which is rooted in the eternal counsel of God but has found fulfillment—or will be fulfilled—at some fullness of time. Mystery, in Pauline usage, has to do with the background and basis of the gospel, and with what the gospel makes possible to those who believe it—deliverance from sin, newness of life, inward and outward healing, answers to prayer, and more. We preach so that God's saving and sustaining action can be experientially known by those who hear and believe us.

We who preach by divine appointment have as our distinct subject area "the mysteries of God." It is important that I say something more here about what we refer to in speaking about "mystery." Gabriel Marcel offered a pertinent statement to aid us when he described the difference between a "problem" and what is essential "mystery." A problem, he explained, is something that can be solved; it is *pro blema*, out there in front of the self, and once a solution to it is found, one can move on beyond it. But a mystery is not something external; a mystery involves us existentially, it confronts and engages and pinches us, it situates us in such a way that we know we must yield to its unmanageable strangeness.[3]

Dr. George Washington Carver used to tell a story about himself that well illustrates this. There was that day, he reported, when he had been meditating on life and nature. He moved from thought to prayer. He asked God, "Mr. Creator [his way of addressing the Almighty], why did you make the universe?" God responded to the query, but it was an admonition to ask for something more in keeping with what his mind might more readily grasp. So Carver revised his question, scaled it down, and asked God why he had made humans. He was told inwardly that he still wanted to know too much. Praying there in his laboratory with his eyes open—his customary way—Carver noticed some peanuts drying on a nearby shelf, and he asked God to tell him the purpose peanuts were created to serve. The Almighty seemed pleased, and told Carver that if he would busy himself to separate the peanut into its many elements, then he would learn much about its uses. So, using what he knew of chemistry and physics, Carver worked and separated the oils, gums, resins, sugars, starches, and acids found in the peanut. In separating the constituent elements of the peanut in this way, Carver was working on a problem, and, over time, his "solution" to the problem posed by the peanut uncovered or discovered or disclosed or invented new uses for the peanut—three hundred new uses, actually— but the mystery of humans and the universe continued to haunt Carver's mind and spirit across the rest of his life. Dr. Carver rightly embraced the mystery of being human in this kind of world, aware that the mystery had embraced him!

Yes, a mystery involves us existentially, because we are embraced by it. We cannot dismiss mystery, because we cannot isolate mystery from our own being. Mystery is something whose utter strangeness and stubbornness forever resist all attempts on our part to domesticate it, dominate it, define it or dismiss it. Life is a mystery! Death is a mystery! The incarnation—the coming of God in Jesus Christ—is a mystery! The resurrection of Jesus from death is a mystery! Our life on this planet involves us in mystery. The Story of God's gracious dealings with us through grace involves us in mystery! We can experience the mystery, but, try as we might, we cannot explain it. We who preach are stewards of the mysteries of God. What we offer and extend through preaching can be experienced but it is more wonderful—filled with what arouses wonder and awe—than we can fully explain.

Dr. Gardner Taylor has told about an experience he and Mrs. Laura Taylor had near the end of his first preaching mission in Australia years ago.[4] They were treated by their host with a visit to the studio of an outstanding Australian landscape artist, a man whose work had earned him a British knighthood. As Dr. Taylor looked about in the studio, his eyes caught sight of a massive canvas on which the artwork was only half-finished. He asked the artist about it. The artist shook his head, a little sadly Taylor thought, and explained that the unfinished picture was to have been a scene he had experienced during a visit to Australia's northern territory, but after much trying he had been unable to depict the real beauty of the scene that had captured him. Taylor saw, in the felt limitation that artist confessed to, a parable of the glory and pain of the preacher: while there is so much that can be seen and known and said about Jesus Christ, he is still a subject too vast to fully capture in our work, because his sacrificial life and work are rooted in "the mysteries of God."

I remember wrestling with the text and meaning of 1 Timothy 3:16 in order to preach on it for the first time. What a declarative and definitive word about the content, center, and circumference of the Christian faith! Notice how the apostle introduces that grand hymn about the incarnate Christ, and how he refers to the facts of our treasured faith as "mystery":

> Without any doubt, the mystery of our religion is great:
> He was revealed in flesh,
> vindicated in spirit,
> seen by angels,
> proclaimed among Gentiles,
> believed in throughout he world,
> taken up in glory.

I also remember my attempts to preach on that great christological hymn that Paul preserved for us in Philippians 2:6–11. In the context of the first-century church this hymn not only proclaimed the mystery of the incarnation and the drama of the saving death of Jesus, but also his present exalted role as cosmic Lord—and the universal homage to him that God has purposed and will surely effect.[5] What a grand and needed word to remind the church about our center of gravity! The

Christ we are sent to preach about is not just Lord of the church; the time is coming when he will be vindicated and acknowledged as Lord of the universe! This truth is one among the many "mysteries of God" entrusted to our telling.

Paul took pride, although humbly, in being God's steward in preaching such truths. Paul stated, "If I proclaim the gospel, this gives me no ground for boasting, for an obligation is laid on me, and woe to me if I do not proclaim the gospel!" He went on to explain, "For if I do this of my own will, I have a reward; but if not of my own will, I am entrusted with a commission" (1 Cor. 9:16–17). That word "commission" could just as well be rendered "stewardship," because behind it is *oikonomia*, a Greek term translated elsewhere as "stewardship." Paul understood himself as one of God's stewards, someone entrusted to handle and herald the gospel, someone whose province in preaching was "the mysteries of God" or, to use Paul's words from his descriptive charge to a group of preachers gathered at Miletus, "the whole counsel of God" (Acts 20:27 RSV).

III

Since this commissioning trust was committed not only to Paul and successive generations of Christian preachers but also to us, our concern should be to live and labor honorably as "good stewards." Paul spelled out some requisites for doing so when he wrote "Think of us in this way, as servants of Christ and stewards of God's mysteries. Moreover, it is required of stewards that they be found trustworthy" (1 Cor. 4:1–2). In a day when publicity blurbs seem demanded for all who seek acceptance in a highly competitive social arena, just how do you want people to think of you? How do you advertise or explain yourself? Paul was eager to be thought of first as *hyperetes*, a "servant," a category whose rich history of meaning includes the notion of "assistant," someone who assists a superior, someone who is secondary to someone else who holds a place of importance.[6] Paul went on, secondly, to include "and steward," using *oikonomos*, which I have already mentioned means "entrusted manager"—in keeping with guidelines supplied by the one who entrusted the appointed task. Then Paul followed up these descriptions with the statement, "Moreover, it is required of stewards that they be found trustworthy" (or, as the KJV renders it, "faithful"). Paul's description here states the necessity for the person assigned a stewardship to "be found" (*heurethe*—discovered, disclosed, seen) as indeed trustworthy. Being called a "steward" is not enough; one must *be* a steward. It is not enough to be called a preacher; one must *be* a preacher. And the true preacher, Paul tells us, honors the commission from God to handle and herald the divine "mysteries," the startling, saving, sustaining truths of the gospel. Stewards are highly privileged persons.

Among the many memorable and insightful cartoons Charles Schulz created in his *Peanuts* series, there is that now-classic one that shows Charlie Brown striking out while at bat. As Charlie walked away from the plate, disgusted with himself, he saw Lucy seated on a nearby bench and lamented to her, "I'll never be a Big-League player! I just don't have it! All my life I've dreamed of playing in the Big Leagues, but I know I'll never make it!" Lucy interrupted Charlie's lament with the comment that he was thinking too far ahead. She suggested that what he needed to do was to set himself some limited, more immediate goals. "Immediate goals?" Charlie asked. "Yes," Lucy replied. She then advised that when he walked out to pitch for the next inning, he should just try to walk out to the mound without falling down!

How I remember the many Charlie Brown moments when disgust filled me after striking out in the pulpit! What preacher hasn't had such moments? After "striking out" many times early in my ministry, I found encouragement in something Aurelius Augustine (AD 354–430), bishop of Hippo, confessed about his preaching efforts. Intent to help a discouraged friend regain inspiration to continue his work with readiness, Augustine wrote *On Teaching the Uninitiated*, and in that treatise admitted his own felt limitations as a preacher:

> For my part, I am nearly always displeased with my discourse. For I am desirous of something better, which I often inwardly enjoy before I begin to unfold my thought in spoken words; but when I find that my powers of expression come short of my knowledge of the subject, I am sorely disappointed that my tongue has not been able to answer the demands of my mind. For I desire my hearer to understand all that I understand; and I feel that I am not speaking in such a manner as to effect that.

> This is so chiefly because intuition floods the mind, as it were,
> with a sudden flash of light, while the expression of it in speech
> is a slow, drawn-out, and far different process.[7]

While each one of us might readily and honestly identify with what Augustine confessed, it is to our shame if we fail to work as diligently at preparing to preach as Augustine continued to do. It is my judgment that in the pulpit work of that noble preacher-theologian, the greatest of the Latin Fathers, we have the best example of the stewardship of preaching since apostolic times. I hardly need to remind you of the extent to which Western Christianity is indebted to Augustine. His book *On Christian Doctrine* was one of the first manuals addressed to preachers to help their stewardship. The fourth section of that manual, which treats preaching style, offers Augustine's methods for handling biblical substance, which he discusses in the first three sections of the book. Please note that Augustine gives more space to treating *substance*, "the mysteries of God"—Scripture—than he does to treating *style*. Augustine wisely keeps "first things first."

Sooner or later one learns that the most fruitful approach to good pulpit work is "keeping first things first," working forthrightly and faithfully to reach those immediate goals that make ascending the pulpit stairs meaningful and promising. One of those immediate goals is an engaging acquaintance with the Bible, the sourcebook of our faith, and the ground plan for our recital; and a second immediate goal is gaining a sound understanding of primary texts from which preaching should issue. The "mysteries of God" entrusted to our handling have come to us by special revelation, and they are documented in that book we know as the Holy Bible.[8]

As stewards of The Word, "The Story," we are expected to study the Scriptures in order to know them, and to understand the Scriptures in order to utilize them properly, mindful of the apostolic injunction: "Do your best to present yourself to God as one approved by him, a worker who has no need to be ashamed, rightly explaining the word of truth" (2 Tim. 2:15). When we are indeed serious in our study, and helped in that task by a hermeneutic that honors the biblical texts as a medium of special revelation, we can be stewards who are biblically informed in our approach and deeply committed in faith as we preach, seeking to share our witness with aptness and appeal under the approval of God who sends us forth. These are some immediate goals that we should seek, and they are goals that we can indeed reach. We need only commit ourselves to reach them.

IV

A trustworthy stewardship as preachers also demands courage to preach in these times when religious pluralism influences the public mind and postmodernism has emboldened many to question our message and the necessity of our work.

Rightly understood, our stewardship as preachers allies us with God in shaping the future: the future of an individual hearer, the future of a particular congregation, the future of a given community, a people group, or a nation. When we address someone's consciousness, making an appeal based on God's concern for them, a possible future opens before them through our witness, a future in which Christ is central as Savior and Lord. It is any hearer's freedom to accept or reject, to question or trust, to affirm or deny.

There is a granted courage by which to preach, and we need it. Courage is that quality of spirit and ability of mind that enables us to face any difficulty, danger, pain, or threatening opposition as we preach, so that fear does not curb the reason and effort to do our work. Courage is that ability, that readiness, to assert ourselves on purpose, to act with purpose, fully set to serve that purpose despite changing conditions or threatening odds.

The courage God grants to his preaching stewards is a courage whose moral edge has been sharpened by biblical truth and godly values. It is a courage whose social component is rooted deep within a personal concern to help people. It is a courage that inspires a creativity which keeps us resourceful and inventive in our work. Yes, to help us handle our task faithfully "in season, out of season" (2 Tim. 4:2 KJV)— or as the New Revised Standard Version rendering puts it, "whether the time is favorable or unfavorable"—God grants us a requisite and resourceful courage to do our work.

This courage to preach is more readily experienced and maintained

when we keep reaching beyond the self to God, when we resist con-
forming to things as they are, and when we remain focused on what we
are sent to do: namely, to live by, report, repeat, and apply the gospel
message. God has an announced vision and prescription for human life;
that vision and prescription stand revealed in the Christian Scriptures.
Our stewardship relates us to that vision, and faithfulness in sharing
that vision brings honor to God and makes us of value in the world.

> "Who then is that faithful and wise steward, whom his lord
> shall make ruler over his household, to give them their portion
> of meat in due season? Blessed is that servant, whom his lord
> when he cometh shall find so doing." (Luke 12:42–43 KJV)

2

The Steward as Recitalist

With my mention of the word "recital," some ears, attuned like mine to the world of music, will immediately recall a concert hall scene with some vocalist, instrumentalist, or team of instrumentalists at work projecting skill-shaped tones, intent to interpret well, honor the composer, and satisfy the audience. They will remember that prideful bow at the close of it all, with the musical deed sealed by applause from enthralled and appreciative listeners. "Recital" is for some of us a word that evokes considerable meaning and remembered joy.

One does not soon forget those recital artists who know how to draw us into the music by their presence and work. Those who know how to achieve that tricky relationship called rapport do it with warmth, integrity, a relaxed bearing, and elan. They know how to involve us in their world of form, beauty, and meaning. I must confess that when the question was raised some years ago, "Is the Solo Concert an 'Outmoded' Institution?" I reacted with an immediate answer: No![1] I know that I was speaking only for myself, but I remain confident that supreme artists will continue among us, and since they know what hangs upon them as representatives and interpreters of music, they will not allow what their very lives foster to become outmoded; they will understandably adapt to circumstances, but always with intent to be active, adept, adequate, advancing the cause of music. There are still artists who know how to make music live for those who listen, and they remain on call. Pianist Imogen Cooper commented recently, "I do know that as long as musicians still have passion in their bellies for what music is all about—and can persevere—then the message [in music] will indeed survive."[2]

This whole notion of recital holds some important insights about preaching at its best. Just as ardent musicians keep recital crowds coming, so ardent preachers continue to claim hearers for their work. When there is a controlling respect for sources, when there is a sense of being God's servant, when there is a commitment to make the "hearing" occasion live for the hearers, and when there is a contagious caring from which it all springs, preaching still shows itself "alive and well."

I

Christian preaching, by its very nature, necessarily involves us in the work of reciting, a mode of address that engages hearers through telling about something, calling attention to some event, and interpreting that event so that the telling influences the hearer's belief and action. Even the most cursory look at the Old Testament narratives about the Hebrew prophets or the New Testament stories about the apostolic company, as narrated in the book of Acts, will readily show that their preaching involved telling people a message, a message that was descriptive, confessional, and functional. The New Testament instances some crucial terms regarding that work of telling The Story: There is that word *exegeomai*, which Luke used to mean "to tell, to declare, to explain, to relate, to report, to narrate, to recite." There is that word *apangello*, which means "to announce, to proclaim." The word *diegeomai* is also used. These three terms all focus upon a statement made about some happening, with concern for the meaning and implications of that happening for the hearer's life.[3]

The use of the word "recital" plunges us immediately into the middle of an ongoing debate in theological circles, especially with respect to what constitutes an Old Testament theology or what can be considered as the unifying center of the Old Testament literature.[4] Gerhard von Rad has suggested that a unifying center is clearly seen when the Old Testament is viewed as Israel's "recital" or "re-telling" (*Nacherzählen*) of her life with God.[5] The recital had to do with how Israel used her historical and prophetic traditions kerygmatically, how the nation applied and reapplied the authoritative message to new settings and changing circumstances in her ongoing history. G. Ernest Wright also called attention to Israel's fondness for recital in his book *God Who Acts*, which he subtitled "Biblical Theology as Recital."[6] In recent years, Walter Brueggemann has emphasized "testimony" as a controlling theme in the Old Testament, with Israel seen at work testifying about her confrontations with God who is "in the fray."[7] The confessional and testimonial character of the Old Testament literature is quite obvious, with Israel holding up to view for changing audiences and under changing skies her recital about God and God's ways with people. The study of Israel's way of reciting or retelling helps us to understand why historical narratives abound in the Hebrew Scriptures. In fact, narratives are so abundant there that we cannot overlook story as the major mode among Hebrews for learning and teaching, the intent being to inform, persuade, remind, confess, testify, celebrate, and give witness.

The narratives we have in the scriptural accounts deal with life from a presentational approach. They show humans in situations and leave no major aspect of human experience untouched. Experiential, artistic in form and style, the scriptural narratives are functional stories gathered and preserved for kerygmatic uses. The stories give us history, a consciousness of God, a knowledge of values, and a focus on moral categories. Holding the elemental and enduring aspects of life to view, the stories mediate revelation; they allow the supernatural to penetrate our earthly order of thought in a popular and engaging manner. The biblical narratives bring us face to face not only with the Jewish concept of authoritative literature but also with the nation's concept about depth learning. The rich and multifaceted stories in the Bible are there because of the need to transmit, interpret, and reinforce religious learning and spiritual values; they are an agency of recital.

II

The Christian preacher is an agent of recital. We who preach are commissioned to tell, transmit, interpret, and reinforce the meaning and implications of The Story recorded in the Scriptures. Paul explained it this way: "For whatever was written in former days was written for our instruction, so that by steadfastness and by the encouragement of the scriptures we might have hope" (Rom. 15:4). This Story of which we are stewards is a Story of sequence, with many periods and personalities of history involved, and a Story of consequence, because believing it gives one "life in his name" (John 20:31). This Story involves reality and revelation, and it is from this resource that the preaching which really matters always issues.

The Story we are sent to recite involves a distinct understanding of God and a crucial understanding of the human self. It is the long and revealing story of how salvation has come to the world. This Story about salvation rightly informs us and readily inspires us; it answers questions—life's deepest. It raises our consciousness to see the things of God, and by its vitality helps us to know those things in depth by letting us experience them. This is how we become witnesses. This Story about which we are sent to speak is not elementary, it is elemental: elemental for affirmation, for witness, for evidence, for argument, for impact, for ethos, and for engagement. This Story is the basis for the faith that saves.

We live our days under the impact of stories. Some of those stories are factual, some are fictional, and some others are "factional," to use that word Alex Haley coined to mean a fictionalization of fact. No day in our lives would be a normal day apart from some story in our consciousness, even if that story only takes shape as fancy in our own imagination. Stories about what has happened, both near at hand and faraway, together with interpretations about their expected effects, shape the tone of our working days, challenge our waking hours, and sometimes delay our sleep. Whether in the form of ready presentiments on television, the blared news notes on radio, or the bold headlines in the daily press, we are impacted daily by stories; our awareness is linked with happenings.

The Story we are sent to tell is a confessional Story about a divine happening with eternal effects for those who accept, believe, and act on it. This confessional Story grants the believer focus, hope, and identity in relation to God and Jesus Christ. This Story began with the determinative acts of God toward the patriarchs in Israel's prehistory, continued with Israel's election by God in the exodus, and involved a covenant God established with Israel as a chosen people. But The Story widened to involve the saving work of Jesus Christ, the formation of the church, the service of the church as the people of God in the world, and God's announced plan to end history through a new beginning made possible with the coming of "a new heaven and a new earth" (Rev. 21:1). Our given Story, then, is a confessional Story about historical events in which God has acted and will act, always forwarding the ends of his divine plan. The Old Testament gives us a basic unit-story from Abraham down to the times of the early prophets, while the rest of Israel's literature repeats and reviews that story in both short and extended treatments.[8] The New Testament gives us the story of Jesus Christ and the church, the prized context of our own personal story as redeemed, called persons. The Gospels tell about the life, death, and resurrection of Jesus Christ, while the book of Acts and the Epistles treat the spiritual and social results that follow belief that his life, death, and resurrection are God's work. The entire Bible is a confessional book that provides an unlimited resource within which to live, search, and discover, and from which to learn, teach, and preach. This confessional Story reports some divine actions, introduces humans to a divine claim, and challenges the reader or hearer to make a faithful response to it all.

Our work as recitalists can be as varied and multiform as the Scriptures themselves. It can involve basic statement, argument, poetry, and even story itself. It can involve analysis, defense, and interpretation of events. It can involve confession and celebration. Our work is to share meaning that elicits faith, and this can be done whether we are reciting events, rehearsing meanings, probing biographies, exploring promises, calling attention to fulfillments, or clarifying divine commands. When our preaching is true to the biblical tradition, when it succeeds in making clear the meanings germane to that tradition, it can elicit faith, give a sense of identification, grant renewal, and be a means to actualize the believer's potential in grace. Paul was pointing to such results when he wrote, "So faith comes from what is heard, and what is heard comes through the word of [*or* about] Christ" (Rom. 10:17).

The whole Bible must inform our work, not just the New Testament. James A. Sanders rightly reminded those of us who preach that "the meaning of the cross can be viewed only from the perspective of the whole Bible. To study the cross or the gospel only in the New Testament is like studying twentieth-century man without taking account of all the centuries of man that have gone into his make-up." He continued, "But the case is stronger than the analogy, for the New Testament itself insists that its rootage is the Old Testament."[9]

Some years ago, in her insightful book on *The Old Testament and the Proclamation of the Gospel*, Elizabeth Achtemeier elaborated on some of the problems the Protestant churches in America experienced when the Old Testament was virtually abandoned and church life was more and more oriented to fragments of the New Testament—or no Scripture at all. With the loss of a vital biblical witness about the mighty acts of God, worship services were divorced from biblical models and centered primarily in human fellowship; folk songs replaced confessional hymns; aesthetic experiences replaced depth communion with God; human opinion replaced an authoritative "Thus says the Lord"; the receiving of sacraments became an expression of congregational togetherness, rather than a remembrance of the Lord's death; and counseling, sensitivity training, and encounter groups were conducted with no biblical reference but rather with totally secularized insights and contemporary exercises; ethical relativism took the place of biblical norms and Christian values. Elizabeth Achtemeier wrote as one who rightly understands the importance of the whole Bible in eliciting faith and shaping a Christian worldview: "This is not a situation to be taken lightly, for unless the church's life is rooted and nourished in the Bible, it has no possibility of being Christian. . . . The Old Testament story looks forward to Jesus Christ; the New Testament remembers him. Without that story the Christian church has no possibility of existence."[10] Achtemeier wrote that book to prod preachers toward a renewed use of the whole Bible in preaching. The fullness of our Story demands a proper use of the whole book.

III

Amos N. Wilder once referred to the narratives of the Old Testament as "a large-scale kind of recital," as indeed they are.[11] A large expanse of time and experiences stands plotted and exposed in those narratives. The Old Testament reveals the self-understanding of the Hebrews and the theology that developed as they interrogated their experiences with Yahweh, who had chosen them as his own agent-people. Those narratives show us a serious view of time and seasons, and an unfolding historical process is nearly always under review in the Hebrews' telling of their life in the world with God. The patterned events reported in the narratives are so ably pictured that one experiences watching a graph of destiny, and not just temporal happenings and successive actions. The biblical narratives are more than structured literary forms arranged in contrived sequence; they are transcripts of living experiences, whether distinctly historical or, in some instances, only "history-like."[12] The narratives have been preserved because of specific characters with remembered experiences from life in actual places and distinct social settings. The stories relate these experiences because of some thematic aspect that needs to be shared for appeal, for teaching, for effect, for guidance. The narratives are all purposive, and predominantly revelatory. Classify them as we will—as saga, epic, romance, tragedy, parable, myth, or whatever—a purpose always underlies the narrative and unfolds for the reader or hearer who is confronted in the telling of it. Each narrative betrays a point of view, a perspective, and helps the reader or hearer to share in it.

Recital preaching that appealingly utilizes the biblical narratives is basically at one with the prevailing style of the biblical materials themselves. In an earlier work, *Designing the Sermon*, I offered some insights on how to preach appealingly from a biblical narrative, how to contemporize and put its message to new use.[13] The concern and appeal was for more of this kind of preaching because it is at one with the cast of the Scriptures themselves, on the one hand, and the most appealing approach for sharing the kerygma, on the other. It is appealing because all of us are like children when it comes to a story, and there is more to this than mere curiosity. Narratives, or stories, are part of our culture, an effective element for our learning and the socialization process that shapes our personal history, our group identity, and even the national character itself. We do not react to stories as a mere influencing phenomenon, but because stories call out to us, challenge us, and make a claim upon us. Storytelling in the pulpit is a practical way to guide the imaging the people do. This is not manipulative, although in the telling we do lead hearers into certain states of mind by the way we present it all. But hearers should be affected by such a telling, since story and perception are interlocked.[14] The appealing use of biblical narratives in preaching can give necessary substance to the imaging people do. What better than a biblical story to widen the parameters of our experience and help us to envision wider possibilities for ourselves?

Recital preaching from biblical narratives gives the hearer a rest from having to follow sometimes heavy-footed topical treatments of the biblical message. To be sure, systematic statements and propositional arguments have a proven place in the preaching task, but biblical stories can also provide the needed themes, strategic insights, and implied argument that elicits faith and deepens it. Preaching from a biblical narrative permits a kind of sideways look at truth, but this is often more effective, because it lets us *see* the truth and not just hear about the truth. The systematic, analytical, propositional approach in preaching is distinctly frontal, whereas the narrative approach is oblique but uniquely gripping. According to the Gospel accounts, Jesus preferred the narrative approach as a preaching and teaching method. So strong was his preference for the method, Mark tells us, that "he did not speak to them except in parables" (4:34a). That is to say, Jesus granted propositional understandings by means of illustrative stories. No wonder "the common people heard him gladly" (Mark 12:37 KJV).

We tend to overlook the fact that most religious insights are best expressed and understood pictorially. There has been some discussion about this in linguistic study circles, with one scholar writing about "Religious Beliefs as Pictures."[15] But as far back as 1938 Ludwig Wittgenstein was discussing this in his teaching. Some students who heard him lecture on religious belief recalled Wittgenstein's treatment of the notion of the last judgment, and his suggestion that the picture influences the behavior of one who believes in it, making that believer risk things on account of that belief. Wittgenstein's point was that a way of seeing leads to a certain way of thinking and acting.[16] Religious statements are quite often pictorial, and people will relate to the pictures they conjure up, sometimes viewing them as literal fact, but always as something clearly seen "in the mind's eye." Picture-speaking is a powerful mode of address, and it is done not only through the direct use of narratives, but also through the strategic use of imagery and well-placed metaphors.

Among the problems that now plague our pulpits is an almost exclusively logical and propositional approach in addressing the human heart. Recital preaching can involve propositional detail, but pictorial preaching honors the whole mind, addressing intellect and intuitive powers at one and the same time. There will always be a place for defining, a place for propositional statements, and a time for the logical ordering of facts and doctrines, but an exclusive use of the propositional approach usually restricts one's preaching to an intellectual function, to the neglect of the hearer's intuitive side. Meaning can be sensed, but without a felt engagement.

Interestingly, the first narrative in the Bible mixes propositional statement and pictorial language. When we read in Genesis 1:1 that "in the beginning God created the heavens and the earth" (RSV), the process of creation is introduced by a pictured activity. A doctrine is taught through a visionary recital. Affirmation and narration are conjoined. The teaching about God as creator is sharpened by the vision that is conveyed in the story. The Creation Story was calculated to grant meaning and engage one's faith. Recital was the Yahwist's natural modality for the educational and religious task. It is not incidental that the Hebrew Scriptures and the Scriptures of Christianity are largely comprised of narratives.

So! Through recital preaching we prod hearers to identify with what the stories present as their witness. We take stories in which biography, autobiography, sociology, and theology conjoin, and let their testimonial power impact the hearer's consciousness for faith and life. We rehearse the lives of earlier persons who made good or bad decisions—acted in wisdom or folly—and reaped from their deeds divine approval or rebuke. We listen anew to promises from God, promises that shape a destiny, sometimes in conditional ways and sometimes unconditionally. Through this preaching we rehearse the ways of God with the proud and the humble, with the poor and the rich. Through our recital preaching hearers can "watch" God rebuke highhanded leaders who use power arrogantly, like Pharaoh and Nebuchadnezzar. We can remind ourselves about the importance of obedience, about morality in the midst of temptations, and about persistence and patience in well-doing.

We learn how to wait as we watch persons being tested by circumstances across time while under heavy anxieties about their lives and their hopes, persons like childless Abraham and Sarah, Hagar as a single parent, Joseph in Egypt, Moses in the desert, Hannah in her barrenness, Naomi and Ruth in their sojourn; the list is near endless.

What are we doing through our recital? We are learning from cases of doubt, human drifting, and gross denial of what is good and right. We are helping people become heartened by stories that pull back the curtain on God's dealings with strategic souls: Isaiah, renewed after a fresh revelation of God's presence in a worship service; Saul of Tarsus, made new and vital after an encounter with the risen Christ. We help our hearers locate themselves under the light of strategic texts and narrated truths. We help our hearers take the road to which truth points them, initiated into biblical meanings, the reality of the sacred, and the available presence of God. What are we about in recital preaching? We let the narratives critique what is routine, rebuke what is inept, challenge what is sinful, show what needs to be seen, and point to what Ralph Waldo Emerson once referred to as "sharp peaks and edges of truth,"[17] supremely the truth as it "is in Jesus" (Eph. 4:21).

The center of our recital is the event of Christ dying on a cross. It is instructive to observe the way Paul utilized the words "cross" and "crucify" as he wrote about the effects of the cross-event for believers. There was always special content given and a specific claim made when Paul used the expression "Christ crucified."

Galatians 3:1 uniquely reflects Paul's focus on the theme of the cross. He there reminds the Galatians of the pictorial way he had preached to them about the death of Jesus Christ, having so reported the scene that they visualized it. This is what those words mean: "It was before your eyes that Jesus Christ was publicly exhibited as crucified!" The translation "publicly exhibited" renders the Greek *proegraphe*, which also means "openly pictured," "graphically expressed." Martin Luther, meditating on this text, commented, "It is as though he were saying, 'No painter can depict Christ as accurately to you with his colors as I have depicted Him with my preaching.' "[18] This same focus on Paul's part is seen in 1 Corinthians 2:1–2, where Paul declares the cross-theme as his major concern while preaching in Corinth. Paul knew what we must always remember in preaching: that divine power stands associated with our recital about the cross of Christ. That power is always experienced in the lives of those who identify with that message as a believer.

The major theme in the New Testament Scriptures is the cross of Christ. Each Gospel account presents the passion story as an essential unit, indeed as the essential nucleus of the entire gospel story. Francis Wright Beare has commented that "it is scarcely too much to say that all the rest is introductory to this."[19] This surely seems to be the case when one is reading the Gospel according to Mark. Again and again the New Testament writers highlight the passion experiences as central in the larger story of Jesus' life. The New Testament is filled with their theological statements about the meanings connected with the suffering and death of Jesus.

This concern to help believers identify fully with recited meanings connected with the suffering, death, and resurrection of Jesus stands behind such Scripture passages as Romans 6:3–7; Galatians 5:24; 6:14; and Colossians 2:11–13, among others, where Paul treats the motif of dying and rising with Christ.[20] The initial recital of this theme can bring someone to faith, while the perennial treatment of this theme by those who preach can help believers increasingly realize what it means to partake of the results that these events make possible. This is the purpose and point of recital with applied meaning. Like Paul, who confessed that his ambition in preaching was "to make everyone see [*photisai*]" (Eph. 3:9), we can preach with concern and skill to illumine those who hear us, helping them to see the truth we hold to their view. This is what recital preaching is all about, and the *seeing is* strategic to our work.

Christian preaching does not neglect the theme of "Christ crucified" (1 Cor. 1:23). Paul made the case for holding this as our central message as recitalists, and he treated the effects of that death from several angles of vision: its effect as redemption (Rom. 3:24), its effect as expiation (Rom. 2:25), its effect as the means for reconciliation (Rom. 5:10), its effect as basis for our justification (Rom. 5:9), and its effect as ransom (1 Tim. 2:6), to list a few. There is a wealth of meanings to be gained from these terms and angles of vision, about which Vincent Taylor, Leon Morris, and John Stott, among others, have written so ably.[21] In his recital about our Lord's passion Paul also outlines the eschatological effects of the death of Jesus. That apostle's relative silence about the historical Jesus does not reflect any disinterest in these details, but rather his overarching concern to explicate the meanings associated with the exaltation of the resurrected Jesus as Christ and Lord. George Eldon Ladd has explained it this way: "All that Jesus in history had meant was included, and enlarged, in the preaching of the exalted one."[22] Preaching about Jesus as Lord (2 Cor. 4:5; Rom. 10:8–10; etc.) deliberately honors his present status as exalted Son and underscores the uniqueness and once-for-allness of his mission as Savior. There are meanings to the gospel message, and it is our task to deal with both that message and its meanings in our preaching.

IV

Given the importance of what we do as recitalists for God, we need to follow a plan that will guarantee a wide knowledge and use of the Scriptures for our preaching. The Bible stands before us whole, offering its wide range of materials for our exploration and use. We who preach should study it all, learn from it all, and use it all. If we are to declare "the whole counsel of God" (Acts 20:27 RSV), there is no refuge from the demand to be familiar with the whole Bible, seeking ever to extend the range of our knowledge about and competence for handling The Story. Familiarity with the Scriptures can lead to encounter with the life current that flows within them when one has felt the power of "the biblical way of speaking," or what Martin Buber described as a genuine "spokenness" (*Gesprochenheit*) that resides in the Scriptures.[23] This encounter with God through canonized texts is not as a detached spectator but as someone being addressed, and who listens! This is the prelude to relevant preaching.

We who preach are recitalists. We have our confessional, witnessing, functional work to do, and we must keep doing that work until all the world has heard The Story. The Story must be shared "as a testimony to all the nations," said our Lord, "and then the end will come" (Matt. 24:14). Preaching has a primary place in making that testimony known, understood, and believed. And our written resource is the Scriptures we have, a resource that is readily relevant and perennially adequate. In connection with this, Gardner C. Taylor has commented that among the most amazing aspects of preaching "is the awareness that the sixty-six books in the canon and particularly the twenty-seven 'pamphlets' in the New Testament have sustained twenty centuries of preaching with not the faintest suggestion of exhaustion."[24] Those who wrote the Scriptures had a passion in their bellies for what The Story is all about. When we who preach have a like passion, and let our lives foster what The Story is about, our preaching will live for those who listen and bear fruit in their lives.

Many years ago, while delivering the Beecher Lectures on Preaching at Yale Divinity School, Phillips Brooks (1835–93) called attention to how a right handling of The Story keeps the preacher in right relations with historic Christianity. "Whatever else you count yourself in the ministry," Brooks advised his hearers, "never lose this fundamental idea of yourself as a messenger."[25] "The identity of the Church in all times consists in the identity of the message which she has always had to carry from her Lord to men."[26] "I am sure," he promisingly declared, "that the more fully you come to count your preaching the telling of a message, the more valuable and real the Church will become to you, the more true will seem to you your brotherhood with all messengers of that same message in all strange dresses and in all strange tongues."[27]

3

The Steward and Rhetoric

Booker T. Washington, founder and first principal of Tuskegee Institute, was unusually successful as a public speaker. Once, in referring to how he planned his speaking, Washington confessed: "When I have an address to deliver, I like to forget all about the rules for the proper use of the English language, and all about rhetoric and that sort of thing, and I like to make the audience forget all about these things, too."[1] What Washington no doubt meant is that rules and rhetoric must become instinct if they are to serve us well, and that one's purpose in speaking must be more absorbing than the formalities involved. Booker T. Washington certainly knew the logic essential to speaking effectively. Nor did he allow himself to forget that logic, despite his stated concern to give the audience "*soul* in an address."[2] One of his biographers tells about a copy of one of Washington's most effective speeches on which he had penned some prompting notes about what to do at certain points of emphasis: he was intent *not* to forget, prompting himself at one point by the word "quiet," at another point by the word "Pause," and at still another place by the word "Force."[3] If Booker T. Washington did "forget" rhetoric, it was only in the sense that he let himself become caught up into its service for his message.

Preaching demands a knowledge of how to use words, how to handle language, how to organize aspects of a subject for proper sequencing, proportion, unity, and clarity. One word describes the system by which all these factors are understood and governed: rhetoric.

Rhetoric has to do with intention and design in speaking. Given the special nature and purpose of preaching, rhetoric is a proper province for our concern. Vocabulary, grammatical relations, and sentence technique are for us no side issues at all. Effective preaching calls for competence among speech levels and word meanings, with which rhetoric deals.

I

A sermon usually begins through abstracting a text; that is, when a truth or theme is drawn from that text.[4] The sermon develops out of the preacher's concentrated thought about one or more features seen in the text, and this selective interest will usually influence the preacher's design for the sermon, the choice of words to be used, and the style of presentation. As an abstraction of a text, the sermon is expected to take what that text has provided and put it all to use in a new setting. The sermon that remains related to its text partakes from the life of the text and can be heard as "word of God." The notion of authority is thus wedded to creativity, so that the preacher's rhetoric becomes marked as something more than self-initiated words.

We can learn so much about this by studying the way the Old Testament prophets went about their speaking task. Sensitive to the truth they were sent to preach, those spokespersons concerned themselves with *how* to preach it and shaped a rhetorical tradition whose influence is still felt in reading their work. The prophets were concerned about means as crucial to ends in their preaching. Their speech forms fall into some obvious patterns, showing us that some of the prophets pursued a formal technique by which to mark their task with dignity and weightiness.

Consider, for example, the formulae the prophets used in introducing their message:

1. There was the initial *Proclamation Notice: něʾum Yahweh*, "says the Lord," or *koh ʾāmar Yhwh*, "thus speaks Yahweh." The hearer was thus informed about the importance of what was about to be uttered.

2. There was, next, the prophet's *Statement of Experienced Authorization to Speak:* "The word of the Lord came [*hāyâ'el*] to me." This prior "hearing" from God was a precondition for their speaking task.
3. There was a *Recognition of Those Being Addressed:* "Hear the word that the LORD speaks to you, O house of Israel" (Jer. 10:1); "Thus says the Lord GOD: Enough, O princes of Israel!" (Ezek. 45:9). The prophets never preached in general, but always with particularity.
4. Then followed the *Message and Its Implications.*

The sermons and oracles of the prophets are revealing rhetorical forms. J. Lindblom commented that "the oracles of the prophets were mostly given a peculiar form. They were as a rule briefly and rhythmically worded."[5] The rhetoric of the prophets embraced a variety of forms: exhortation, dialogue, debate, consolation, reproach, promise, historical retrospect, parable, rebuke, song, dirge, lament, poetry, satire.[6] Whatever the rhetorical form, the message germ was clear, and the prophets used considerable freedom in expanding that message and in applying it. Whether the setting was a street gathering, a court scene, a temple or sanctuary service area, or somewhere else; whether they spoke with brevity or at length, the prophets sent forth their words with a sense of authority to do what they were doing, intent on achieving their end. Isaiah 55:10–11 is a statement to embolden that prophet's confidence that his words would effect an end, and that passage is one of the most comprehensive statements in the Bible about the power and effects of the spoken word of God.

Like the ancient prophets, the commissioned preacher receives a word from God and has the freedom to share that message as the setting and one's personal gifts determine. A proper introduction is still crucial, as is a conceptual pattern that fits the needs of those being addressed by the word. Like the prophets, we speak under God's anointing when we have listened to what God directs us to say. That listening is associated with the prayerful, patient "hearing" of a text. The result of "having heard from the Lord" makes the perennially difficult task of preaching more readily managed. As the prophet Amos once voiced it, "The Lord GOD has spoken; who can but prophesy?" (Amos 3:8b). The preparation to preach, then, rightly involves a close, firsthand entrustment of the self to some text of Scripture.

II

The texts of Scripture are best viewed not as mere document-texts but as Voice-texts. Something does stand documented in the Scriptures, as we know, but the written texts are more than mere documents: God speaks through them, which is why we refer to the Scriptures as "the Word of God." The documentary aspect of the texts allows us to trace details—details of history, culture, language factors, and so forth, but the revelatory aspect is also active by means of the record to make its lively claim upon us. The documented details press the preacher to be a disciplined student, while the patient listening to the Voice in the text requires a devoted suppliant.

The biblical text holds an intentionally prepared and preserved message.[7] The texts are a kind of "stand-in" for the authors in their absence, each author being a potent presence through the intentional sharing of the message. All of this is involved in facing a text. The text comes to us from the past, but it represents something more than the past; it does much more than merely open previous history to our gaze; because of its provenance the biblical text addresses us in our history and speaks to us about a needed hope. "For whatever was written in former days," Paul explained, "was written for our instruction, so that by steadfastness and by the encouragement of the scriptures we might have hope" (Rom. 15:4).

The immediate goal of textual study is to understand the intention behind the text and the message in the text. The writing reflects a purpose, and behind that purpose is a writer who was part of a people's history and who used that people's language (and distinctive dialect) to deal with them on understood levels of meaning. The writer's rhetoric stands exposed in the terms and expressions and style used to share insights and make an impact. Sometimes the writer's intention can be immediately perceived through some situation that is being addressed, but sometimes we must work hard through research to "catch up" with the writer and the original audience. A case in point is the research necessary to understand the code the writer of the book of Revelation utilized to strengthen his audience in their faith, hope, and fortitude. Every serious student of the Scriptures soon learns that some biblical writings are easier to read and understand than some others. When we as preachers examine texts, we will be concerned about the writer's vocabulary, the writer's assumptions and beliefs, the writer's techniques and literary forms, and we will seek to move from the surface structure of the text to the depth meaning it holds. The surface structure of a text involves its physical characteristics, wording, grammar, and syntax, while its depth meaning involves the function and forcefulness of the textual form, together with its relationship to the entire book that "situates" it.

Books abound of late that deal with the literary forms in the Bible, a knowledge of those forms being strategic for interpreting texts.[8] There is indeed so much more that one gains from Scripture study when one knows how textual form relates to textual function. Having earlier considered the form called "story," a well-known literary category, I want to mention three additional descriptive categories not usually treated except by those who work as semanticists: "statements," "expressions," and "prescriptives." In the biblical stories, the narratives, the writers have given us reports of happenings, as we have discussed. In their many "statements," those writers have given us sentences that assert or affirm certain facts. In their "expressions," the biblical writers have let emotion and impulse show through, while in their "prescriptives" they have given direction about something to be done.[9] Stories abound in the Bible because so much has happened in and for the history of the people of God. Statements abound in the Bible because the faith involves facts to be understood and believed. Expressions abound in the Bible because the writers had deep feeling as they did their witnessing, writing, and reporting. Prescriptives abound in the texts because the writers knew that the imperative and the indicative must always relate in the experience of grace and obedience.[10] In addition to a recognition of midrash, paraenesis, topoi, creeds, blessings, doxologies, diatribe, aphorism, parable, chiasm, admonition, and so forth, the preacher needs to recognize texts that are statements, or expressions, or prescriptives, since these are fundamental categories that serve a functional end.

As we examine texts, opening ourselves to the "sound" of the truths voiced in them, we soon discover distinct differences in the language skills and rhetoric of the writers. The differences between their sentence structures have been noted and assessed again and again by alert grammarians.[11] The sentences of Paul rush like torrential rains; they are filled with participial phrases, relative clauses, parenthetical asides, and strategic digressions. Luke differs greatly from Paul, given his rich vocabulary, highly cultured tone, and distinctive literary touches; Luke was a formalist, if ever there was one. The author of the letter to the Hebrews matches Luke in these abilities and traits as a writer. John's writings show a habit pattern of poorly connected clauses, while Mark's Gospel is filled with pictorial participles, double negatives, broken clauses, ever present adjectives and exclamations, all used to achieve vivid narration. The writings that bear Peter's name match what we have come to know about the man: they are impulsive, spicy, rushing, and full of feeling. All of these writers had access to the known religious terminology and theological concepts treasured in the early church, but each writer's expressiveness is unique.

Let us return for a moment to Paul and his rhetorical style as writer. A primary example of his often difficult structuring of sentences is found in Ephesians 1:3–14. This passage is crucial in preaching an expository series on that letter. It is a thanksgiving section, by classification, and it sets forth the initial statement of the theme about unity in Christ. The style is a conglomerate flow that has awkward features. Essential accents in the message are being conveyed, but *one must discover those accents*, because Paul's style has overshadowed them.[12] The sentence lacks the symmetry one expects, yet it is jam-packed with rich theological substance. Perhaps Paul's thought rushed so that he tripped over himself while working with his amanuensis.

I have mentioned Ephesians 1:3–14 because it is but one of many such sentences with which a preacher will have to wrestle in planning an expositional series of messages on that letter. Here are some of those other sentences:

1:15–23	3:1–7	4:17–19	5:28–30
2:1–7	3:8–12	4:20–24	6:1–3
2:11–12	3:14–19	5:3–5	6:5–8
2:14–16	4:1–6	5:18–23	6:14–24
2:19–22	4:11–16	5:25–27	

A good translation helps in reading these sentences, but the reader will still have problems to solve. At least one of those sentences, 2:14–16, is of a hymnic cast, a fact that further enriches the thrust of the writer's rhetoric.[13]

One is helped in locating the depth structure of a text by seeing it in relation to the sectional theme within which it is embedded. As a part of its context, a text is either primary or subsidiary; it either asserts or explains something and is seldom, if ever, incidental or a mere appendage. A close, prolonged exposure to any text finally makes this evident.

We have to remember this when we face texts that are strange to our present way of thinking and speaking. The scenarios in the book of Revelation are potent in their impact, once they are understood, but who is not appalled by the chaotic diversity of interpretations about how that Apocalypse and its imagery should be viewed or its meaning applied? Apocalyptic and eschatological terminology and images are part of a language-form of evocation and encounter, a code language used during crisis times, during critical periods when everything meaningful to believers seemed about to be lost, or when some judgment appeared at hand.[14]

The motifs of apocalyptic hark back to the Old Testament period, and even further. Amos N. Wilder has described much of its language as "archetypal and prepersonal," "dynamic and ultrarational."[15] This form of biblical rhetoric demands the greatest care in approach, analysis, and application. We must not avoid Scriptures clothed in such rhetorical garb as we plan and carry out our preaching task, but neither should we make apocalyptic and eschatology the major emphasis in our preaching. Apocalyptic and eschatological texts must be treated because they are a part of the biblical Story of which we are stewards, but let us treat those texts without historicizing their spiritual message or spiritualizing their historical motifs.

Problems linked with eschatology and apocalyptic images keep us reminded of our need, as interpreters, for help from professional biblical scholars. Our studies in seminary were at best only an initiation into readiness as interpreters of the Scriptures. Mature professional scholars in the biblical and historical disciplines can, through their work, help us to gain skill in hermeneutical procedures and to make reasonable judgments about the meaning of texts. Their published offerings about texts can help us to double-check our own thinking about specific texts. We all need help when some text stumps us. Acts 8:30–31 mentions a Nubian chamberlain who realized that he was stumped as he read a passage in Isaiah; it was a passage that could bless his life, but until Philip the evangelist came and answered his questions about that text, that blessing eluded him. We who preach need professional scholars as that Ethiopian eunuch needed Philip. Scholars and preachers need each other. Scholars and preachers hold varying combinations of talents, skills, outlooks, and interests. Both scholars and preachers are stewards of The Story, and both have a responsible assignment to serve and bless the church and world.

The Scriptures will forever make demands upon us as preachers. There is the demand to look into the writings, and to listen to what is being said in them. In our looking, we must observe rhetorical forms, and in our listening we must be attentive to The Voice that speaks. A true listening helps us declare a message with certitude and conviction, having defined that message with clarity.

Many preachers have given their witness about the time in their life when the duty of study became a task of joy for them, the time when all of their energies became so attuned and focused that they felt readied for preaching. Englishman John Henry Jowett (1864–1923) was such a witness. Jowett's biographer said that "he loved to take a word, as an entomologist takes a moth, and having, figuratively speaking, stuck a pin through it, subject it to a long microscopic examination."[16] Jowett brooded over the biblical writer's rhetoric while shaping his own rhetoric to preach the truth seen in the text.

It was the same with Scotsman Arthur John Gossip (1873–1954). As Gossip read his Bible, each text would light up from the gleam of something he remembered from life experiences. In one of his Warrack Lectures, Gossip told how something he had read thirty years earlier suddenly made a certain text come alive for him; he was blessed by an idea "which all that time had lain dust laden lumber in my mind," but then that idea "rushed at a text, threw on it just the light that I required; and, though I say it, there was a quite admirable sermon forming itself."[17] Gossip understood by experience what it means for preaching when "deep calleth unto deep" (Ps. 42:7 KJV).

African American Gardner C. Taylor is still another witness. This admirable preacher, whose exemplary pulpit work is well known across the English-speaking world, has often expressed his dependence upon biblical content as ready resource for preaching. While giving the Beecher Lectures at Yale, Taylor advised his hearers that "anyone who will open himself or herself to the revelation of God contained in the Bible will find endless preaching, better still, will be found by it, which demands to be delivered of the preacher by pulpit presentation." He continued, "anyone who will undertake systematic reading of the Scriptures, day by day, will find the Living Word leaping up out of the words of the Scriptures. One who does this will often be startled at how directly and immediately the Bible addresses our own life and that of our time."[18] Here also is his advice: "[C]atch the sounds and sights and smells of the accounts recorded in the Bible. Enter as much as you can into the climate of each scene. Let the imagination and the mind work at the same time. Hear in the words of the Biblical record, the long, solemn, and yet tender love call of the Everlasting God aimed at His erring and straying creation."[19] Small wonder that Taylor perennially shapes sermons that match the character and claims of the biblical texts to which he surrenders his heart, thus to preach as he does with intention, biblical insight, rhetorical artistry, and spiritual engagement.

III

E. David Willis has written about how John Calvin (1509–64) shaped his rhetoric in keeping with his sense of responsibility.[20] Intent to balance the usual treatment of Calvin as a logician (the first Protestant to shape a system of doctrine) with that reformer's other accomplishments and assets, Willis explains how concerned Calvin was to wed the biblical content he had mined with just that rhetorical form needed to enhance its reception when taught and preached. Calvin, influenced as he was by the example of Augustine before him, did not separate rhetoric from relevant preaching and theology. Calvin laid stress on spiritual inquiry, mental diligence, and word adequacy, and toward all three of these he worked "strenuously and thoroughly."

John Wesley (1703–91) also spoke and wrote about the strategic importance of words in preaching. While insisting that change in the human heart can be wrought only by God, Wesley did believe that the work of preaching is essential prelude to the work God alone can do.[21] Wesley advised his ministers to be sensitive to the hearer's need and have sound reasons for addressing that hearer in a particular manner.[22]

The biblical word is given to us, but we must structure the sermon by which the textual message can be stated and applied to the lives of those who hear us. This is our responsibility, and to be at our best in this we must remain disciplined by study, meditation, and prayer, always under the tutelage of God. Morgan Phelps Noyes has commented on this: "The truth is that the preacher must come at his message by a double process. He must *work* laboriously for it, using all the resources of the spiritual and intellectual life in his search for truth. At the same time, he must *receive* it. After he has mastered facts and principles, certain convictions master him, perhaps in moments of relaxation when he is not at work on them, and these convictions become the framework of the message he must speak. He is at least sure that they are the Word of God laying hold upon him."[23]

It is necessary that we concentrate on words as we plan and do our preaching: the words of the biblical text that informs us, and the words we will need to recast the message in the text for application in the lives of our hearers. The meaning and message in the text should justify the rhetoric chosen for the sermon based on that text. No rhetoric must be used that obscures the awesomeness and allure of God's Word. Arthur John Gossip lamented that some preachers in his time had been guilty of doing that, going to their pulpits "using great words with little meaning."[24] But the other extreme must also be avoided: treating great meanings with woefully inadequate words.

The biblical text tells us *what* to preach, but it does not tell us *how*. The "how" is a matter of personal manner and divine help, nature and grace. Personality lends a clue, allowing one to plan and deliver the sermon in keeping with individual giftedness. Handling the message has its own aural and visual dynamic, the preacher's persona being part of it all, so that spiritual vision is often mediated by individual vitality in the service of the Word. Effective sermon rhetoric, then, follows from our seeing, feeling, planning, and saying—on God's orders and to God's glory. T. Harwood Pattison put it this way: "The true preacher can be known by this, that he deals out to the people his life—life passed through the fire of thought."[25]

4

The Steward and Ritual

I

Our work as preachers involves us in what across the centuries have become some ritualistic procedures. There are many ritual elements connected with the setting and task of preaching, and we who preach must understand the meaning, importance, and effects of those elements.

First, *preaching is an authorized activity.* The person who preaches does so as an "ordained" person, someone endorsed by a church body, and thus stands linked with certain responsibilities and rights that mark him or her as a ritual figure whose presence and work carry considerable sign value.

It is but a commonplace to remark about the sign value of the preacher. That sign value is further heightened by the preacher's commitment, style, charisma, education, services, community involvement, and any legends that gather around his or her name. The very title "Reverend" projects such sign value. Out in public circles, feelings of respect are stirred in many when someone known to be a "Reverend" appears, and eyes move to take in the person so addressed. The clerical collar is ritualistic and has profound effects, as do the proverbial dark suit, white shirt, and subdued-color necktie in those circles where the preacher is still expected to honor some distinct style of appearance when in public.

Writing with reference to British life and customs, Englishman Russell Brain commented:

> When it is desirable that we should think of and feel towards particular individuals or classes of individuals in a special way, society tends to give them distinctive clothes, or uniforms. The effects of a uniform are both subtle and profound. A judge is not merely an elderly lawyer wearing a bizarre head-dress and a kind of overcoat dating from the remote past. His strange costume, because it is different from the clothes anyone else wears today, symbolizes his exceptional social function and powers; hence all who deal with him are confronted with an embodiment of society. The judge in court is something different in fact and feeling from the same man encountered on a social occasion. His professional persona is socially valuable, and his perceptual equipment contributes materially to it. The same is true of the priest, the policeman, and the postman, each in his different way.[1]

Society associates certain meanings with certain functions and with certain ways of dressing. Miles Mark Fisher has documented the way black slave preachers dressed in relation to their sacred ministries.[2] Usually there was more to their full-dress style than a vain concern for finery in clothes. It was their belief that the spiritual leader should look different from the usual workday appearance; the better clothes marked out the preacher's difference as a changed figure and a God-called spokesperson. The different distinctive dress was a declaration of devotion; it established a mood and pointed to a higher order than the routine. The preacher's clothes thus reflected religious feeling, on the one hand, and a religious responsibility, on the other. In this connection, Fisher cited part of a certain African American spiritual:

> I see brudder Moses yonder,
> and I think I *ought* to know him,
> For I know him by [he clothes] *his garment*,
> *He's a blessing* [Dere's a meeting] here to-night.[3]

But the regard black slaves exhibited toward representative dress in religious life is far wider and earlier than their history. The biblical culture reflects it in the priestly attire, and Psalm 29:2 holds a line that can be understood as an encouragement for special dress during worship.

There the call to worship invites the worshipers to dress in "festive array," that is, vestments that match the purpose of the gathering. We are face to face here with ritual, and with the sign value of a particular way of dressing. The robing of a choir to sing and the robing of the minister to lead worship and preach have to do with ritual and sign value.

Second, in addition to the sign value of the preacher's role as authorized spokesperson, there is the ritual element of *preaching from sacred texts* found in the church's special book, the Holy Bible, a book that bears the Word of God.[4] The texts used in preaching from the Bible are essential to a hearer's "rite of passage," as it were, into the experience of salvation. Paul's statement in 1 Corinthians 1:21 asserts the preacher's role in that process: "God decided, through the foolishness of our proclamation, to save those who believe." And Paul's words in Romans 10:14–15a are of a similar cast and meaning: "But how are they to call on one in whom they have not believed? And how are they to believe in one of whom they have never heard? And how are they to hear without someone to proclaim him? And how are they to proclaim him unless they are sent?"

Third, there is *the ritualistic import of the sanctuary space and architecture* where our preaching is done.[5] In fact, Patrick J. Quinn has explained that a "building becomes architecture only when it becomes ritual."[6] That the pulpit area is a special place is well known and diligently respected. Ascending the pulpit stairs is not just walking up some steps. The pulpit space is a particularized territory of action, a raised section whose higher level in the sanctuary not only makes it readily visible to all but also suggests higher meanings from what happens there. The rich symbolism associated with a pulpit is far too complex for broad treatment here; it will suffice to report and remember that what we do in that sacred space as preachers must relate directly and without distortion to our authorization and responsibility to be there. As regards that authorization and responsibility, our ordained role bespeaks a community relationship between the people in the pews and ourselves. When we are understood, seen, and received by them as authorized agents, we preachers become part of a special process of happenings for and in their lives, and by our work there can be a deepening of that relationship; there can be a reinforcement of beliefs, a sharing of understandings, the granting of explicit guidance, the mutual reception of divine grace, and cooperativeness in ministry.

II

As preachers, we are charged with speaking "the Word of the Lord." Paul W. Pruyser has referred to that spoken word as one of the "numinous noises of worship."[7] We make our numinous noise to open meanings to our hearers. We are authorized to voice "distinct notes" (1 Cor. 14:7), that is, The Story, by which persons are addressed, their hearts engaged, their hopes centered, and their living directed.

The power of preaching involves ritual, but something more than ritual. That power is best served when our preaching is an all-out action that includes feeling, gestures, and a full openness. This means that what the watching listener sees (our gestures, movement, body language) will register its impact along with what the listener hears (our words, inflections, rhetorical factors). This combination of impacts has been referred to as the "duality of communication."[8] Phillips Brooks referred to this combination of impacts when he explained that "preaching is the bringing of truth through personality."[9] Both word and action make pulpit work inviting, letting us preach as whole persons and letting our hearers be totally engaged.

Preaching is ritualistic, but it is more than ritual. It is a verbal manifestation that conveys mediated meaning and mediated Presence.[10] Those who hear our words are candidates for both immediate and lasting effects, because the moment of hearing is a special time (*kairos*) with spiritual elements and meanings that can give content to the rest of one's time (*chronos*). Preaching that is true to its purpose promotes and assists what Douglas Horton liked to describe as "the divine incursion."[11] This is the minister's task within the context of worship, since it is in worship, to quote Horton again, that "the deathless contacts which give meaning to existence are discovered and sustained."[12]

Given the nature and importance of our assignment, it is imperative that we maintain a disciplined commitment as we live. That we who preach are associated with a sign value means that a crown has been placed above our heads; maintaining a disciplined commitment as we live, by which I mean a durable walk with God, we show our desire to grow tall enough to wear that crown.

There is no substitute for a disciplined commitment to God. Jesus referred to this as living with a "single" eye (Matt. 6:22; Luke 11:34

KJV). Such a commitment grants a persuasive intensity that gives depth to one's living and dimension to one's ministry. Knowing what we are called and sent to do, we should do it, and we should do it as committed persons. This whole matter has to do with keeping our self-hood surrendered to spirituality, and keeping our role related to divine realities. Only so will our preaching be more than mere ritual. Margaret Mead once described ritual as that which is repetitious but which is different from the ordinary, possessing "an extra degree of intensity" and "high affective tones."[13] Preaching has these elements when Holy Spirit and human spirit are in agreement and allied in work.

It is possible to speak about God and Christ, even from Scripture, without a right motivation, due sincerity, and a right standing with God. J. L. Austin, writing about hypocrisy in another connection, pictured two crooks engaged at cover jobs in order to carry out a deeper and different intention. One crook was cleaning windows, while the other one was cutting trees, both engaging in effective pretense as they "cased the place" they intended to rob. The faultiness was not in what each one did (cleaning windows, cutting trees) but what he did it as.[14] Moral insincerity blocks the mediation of grace. Role orientation is never enough for purposeful, grace-filled preaching. The preaching that truly matters includes more than role filling; it has to do with biblical meanings, a right motivation to preach, and a sustained relationship with God.

Franz Kafka wrote about his vision of a large city at night in which just a few people were awake. Kafka likened it to a military encampment in which everyone is asleep except a few guards on duty keeping watch. Asking why the few are still awake when all the others in the city are asleep, Kafka answered, "Because someone must be watching, someone must be there."[15] We who preach owe it to those who hear us, and to our Lord, who called us to be that someone who watches, ready to speak a trusted word as a trustworthy person.

III

Ritual shows its value in the way it helps to preserve and pass on meanings in life. Ritual captures the past, but it does more. It makes meanings concrete; it gives them a present tense, so that those meanings can be comprehended in a certain way, at strategic times, and in select places.

As a ritual that is repeated but is expected to bear "an extra degree of intensity" and "high affective tones," preaching can help hearers to apprehend the things of God. When the preacher is more than a ritualist, when he or she exudes in character and service the contagious flavor of the divine, then those who hear the preaching can be carried beyond ritual to experience the reality toward which ritual points. Both preacher and people are in trouble when preaching deadens into routine work, when it is experienced by both as tedium rather than as Te Deum. There is an integrity and invitational power in the Word that God sent to be shared with the world, and God is still eager to bless the work of those who commit themselves fully to the task of sharing it.

The prophets used a ritualistic formula as they did their work. Consider that ever-present declaration "Thus says the Lord," which was spoken either as an introductory statement or as a concluding seal to their message. That ritualistic formula was to mark the message indelibly as Yahweh's very own. Jesus initiated a ritualistic formula that differed from that of the prophets, again and again employing the words "Amen, Amen [or "Verily, verily"] I say to you" to introduce and give emphasis to what he was about to say as an authoritative word.[16] Unlike the prophets, Jesus as Lord did not need to appeal to the divine name. Evangelist Billy Graham regularly appeals to a higher authority while preaching when he uses that ritualistic statement "The Bible says," a statement one of Graham's biographers has called "the most common phrase of his collected sermons."[17] That ritualistic statement not only declares his source of authority but elicits a certain feeling tone as well; it is a word ritual that has strategic meaning and sign value. But whether we preach with or without such a ritualistic formula, every sermon we deliver ought to report what God has sent us to say on his behalf. Preaching, rightly understood, is always God's gracious invitation to hearers, and therefore must have God's message in it. Along with the ritual, but surely beyond it, as David H. C. Read once voiced it, "you listen to a sermon expecting grace."[18]

5

The Steward and Reality

Addressing seminarians and pastors at Yale Divinity School many years ago, John Kelman reminded them that while some persons go to church to be socially respectable or to comfort their conscience, some others go to church because they desire what the church has to offer them: real help for life in this real world.[1] "In this word reality," Kelman insisted, "we find the root of the matter."[2] We who preach can offer that real help if we are on business for the real and true God and faithfully speak God's word with real concern to meet real human needs. That word "reality" explains not only the root of preaching but also the fruit expected from preaching. Real preaching has a distinct ring to it, and a definite power in it. Real preaching will not be sterile, abstract, arrogantly eloquent, nor terrifyingly out of touch with life as people know it.

I

Real preaching is rooted in *the realities of The Story of which we are stewards.* The Story involves characters who are real. The plot is real. The story line is about salvation history, with a real God who has responded with passionate concern toward erring humans to rescue the perishing and care for the dying. The vitality of the preaching tradition is most surely felt when that divine concern is highlighted, when we who preach can point with convictional knowledge as witnesses of that salvation in our own experience.

Jesus spoke often about God: not as an ideal or a mere regulating idea, but rather as an actively responsible and responsive Father who wills the best for the human family. God is a fact, not a mere idea or ideal. To Jesus, God was the first of all facts, if you will accept my putting it that way. I do so because I was impressed many years ago by a sermon of Wade Robinson about Jesus as "a Radical." Robinson explained that he was not using the term "radical" to classify Jesus as a headlong destructionist intent to make arbitrary changes nor as someone out to assail other people. He explained that his application of the word "radical" to Jesus was in honorable recognition of Jesus as "one who lived in connection with the *root* principles which underlie existence" and who therefore knew and "announced God as the first of all facts."[3]

Preaching lives in the reality that God *is*, "and that he rewards those who seek him" (Heb. 11:6b). These are root principles for our work. The Story we are sent to tell is no human fiction; it deals with the facts about the compassionate God who has demonstrated love for us in sending Jesus to save us. This is a key element in a Christian worldview, and it is germane to the meaning that gives value to the whole human scene. To help people know and understand this reality is to help them go beyond sight and sound and gain strength to handle with dignity the heavy weight of the human condition. Real preaching readily affirms that God is and that he rewards those who seek him. Real preaching does not deny paradox or overlook tragedies; it does not look indifferently at necessity and circumscribing circumstance. It faces reality, things as they are—human pain, sickness, disease, sin, distresses, calamities, personal and social evil—but always with concern to face them in the light of God's reality, the history of God's mighty acts, God's promises, and God's offered help. Real preaching helps persons to connect with the life that underlies existence and outlasts the limitations of any present state or condition.

As preachers, our own contact with this undergirding life will betray and evidence itself in many ways. For one thing, that contact will provide a plus element in our own experience. For another, there will be some spillover from it that people will sense from our demeanor, our service to them, and our leadership in worship. As for the leadership we are expected to provide during worship, Willard L. Sperry wrote:

> The reality required in worship is double in its nature. There will be first of all the objective truthfulness of the propositions and transactions of the act of worship. Then there will be our sincere subjective response to this truth.[4]

Staying with The Story we are sent to recite helps to guarantee that "objective truthfulness," and disciplined living allows the real power within that Story to break through in our example.

Real preaching, then, must be described as a message of grace, and real preachers are best described as agents of grace. The message about grace is preached to disclose, describe, and offer the new direction God has opened to us through forgiveness of sins and renewal of life in Christ Jesus. Thus our transcendent task. In real preaching, we offer something more than a mere theological statement. Ours is a living and lively word about the goodness, grace, and faithfulness of God. We preach to call hearers to experience that real and "abundant life" Jesus promised. We preach to "open people upwards" so that spiritual reality can be experienced deep within, where real life begins, takes shape, and is nurtured. Ours is the word about this real and gracious gift of salvation in Jesus Christ. Our work as real preachers is not merely to deal with the nature of what is religious in human experience, but to help hearers to experience God's grace, and to remain in favor with God and others.[5] This distinction is imperative in all real preaching. As Helmut Thielicke has explained, Christian preaching involves letting persons "meet the decisive, active Word," a word that "strikes us as an effectual Word . . . [which] breaks off the old existence and starts a new one, bringing sins to light and forgiving them, changing God's rejection into an acceptance which gives [one] a new future and makes [one] a new creature in the miracle of the Spirit."[6]

Real preaching *highlights that divine grace which deals radically with human sin.* Such preaching provides a catalyst for a happening, a redemptive happening. It is a signal of God's mercies. It helps hearers to see: to see the goodness and graciousness of God and to see humanity as loved enough to be forgiven—and guided.

II

Real preaching takes strict account of the real moral and religious climate and the prevailing conditions of any setting in which our witness is to be given. It is imperative that our pulpit work address the prevailing assumptions and beliefs by which the happenings in our times are determined. Samuel H. Miller was addressing this need when he wrote: "Preaching which assumes that proclamation is all that is necessary, disregarding the nature of contemporary consciousness, I think is too facile and too arrogant to commend itself as more than an ecclesiastical presumption."[7]

In preparing to preach, we must seek to know what dominates the imagination of our hearers and to identify the loyalties to which their energies and time are being given. It might well take us a while to discover the right answers to these questions, but we must try, and we must try until we succeed. What are men and women of our time thinking, really? What are men and women of our time seeking, really? What is the real spirit of the times now upon us? What extremes are prevalent, and why? What tensions lurk menacingly between those extremes? By what perspectives are our modern and postmodern "understandings" determined? What mean the secularity, the relativisms, the proneness to raise questions and debate all possible answers to those questions? What does it augur for us that there is such a widespread loss of any felt need for accountability? Scripture tells us these are symptoms of a diseased human condition that points to our need for help from beyond ourselves.

The Story of which we are stewards tells about that help, and that such help is readily available. The present times are dark, with an acknowledged eclipse of faith, a crisis of belief, the reduction of biblical certainties to a psychologized religion, and a never-ending quest of multitudes to find something larger than themselves with which to identify. Joseph Fort Newton once commented in print that when new theories of knowledge and sad life conditions make for a tangled time, setting the skyline back, preaching is not hurt but helped; he added that the light of preaching shines best when the skies are dark.[8] We do not preach to preserve a culture or to protect our world. We preach to create a new order, to introduce hearers to God's will for us. We must preach to help people see reality as God wills it for us. Our work is a sign of that reality. What a trustworthy assignment and needed task! As Willard Brewing has put it, speaking about the preacher: "Who else encompasses the whole universe, seen and unseen, in life's analysis? Who else measures life, not in scales of material, temporal values, but in terms of eternal treasures?"[9] Yes, what a trustworthy assignment and all-important task!

III

But alas! Over against the realities associated with The Story we have been entrusted to preach, there is another reality with which we must deal—and daily: *the reality of our own selfhood*. We take our stand, intent to speak our word, and public stress and psychic strain make our message muddled. We want to tell The Story with fervor as well as in faith, but a strange coolness and felt detachment prevail within. We try to draw upon what we have seen and known and to speak about those matters with clear thoughts and persuasive speech, yet something inside blurs it all, and the desired clarity, poise, and energy seem strangely absent. No preacher moves very far along the road of service before realizing the need to resist sinning and to deal with the problems of tiredness, psychic strain, and just plain human limitations, what Harry C. Howard once referred to as "the incompleteness that inheres in human nature."[10]

Dr. John Hope, while president of all-male Morehouse College, said in a chapel talk to the students there, "It's an awful feeling, young gentlemen, after a day's work, it's an awful thing to have a feeling as if you've just been squeezed of everything you have."[11] Sooner or later, every earnest preacher knows that feeling. Although there is the necessity for the preacher's work, the gracious fact of a calling to do that work, the presence of gifts graciously bestowed for that service, some wisdom garnered from experience, and perhaps some margin of influence because of that experience, over it all falls the shadow of the preacher's own frailty and incompleteness. Paul understood this and remarked about it in 2 Corinthians 4:7–10:

> But we have this treasure in clay jars, so that it may be made
> clear that this extraordinary power belongs to God and does

not come from us. We are afflicted in every way, but not crushed; perplexed, but not driven to despair; persecuted, but not forsaken; struck down, but not destroyed; always carrying in the body the death of Jesus, so that the life of Jesus may also be made visible in our bodies.

The Story we tell is about God's great deeds, not our own. Whatever transcendent power stands associated with ministering for God belongs to God, not to us.

What I am saying here underscores the need for a right view of ourselves as *human, mortal,* for a humility to match the greatness of our work, and for a trust in God to match its weightiness.

1. Humility becomes us because *our personal gifts are limited.* That is a reality. No one of us has all the gifts to make a ministry perfect and entire, lacking nothing. We must each see and understand ourselves as but part of a larger whole. A variety of ministries is represented, reflected, and realized as we each do our work, and the comprehensiveness of "the ministry" embraces us all. What some cannot do, others can, and each one's work relates to that of all the others. Paul stated it this way: "Now there are varieties of gifts, but the same Spirit; and there are varieties of services, but the same Lord; and there are varieties of activities, but it is the same God who activates all of them in everyone" (1 Cor. 12:4–6).

2. Humility becomes us because *our individual effectiveness is limited.* The reality is that no one preacher's handling of the gospel draws everyone who hears it. There is at work in church life, as in all of life, the law of attraction and appeal. Those who follow some great leader will inevitably be measured against that leader's record, natural gifts, and demonstrated vision, and they must sometimes work hard to gain and hold the allegiance of members who were first drawn to the giftedness and appeal of their predecessor in ministry. The proverbist was indeed wise in saying, "A man's gift maketh room for him, and bringeth him before great men" (Prov. 18:16 KJV), but always that circle is a limited and restricted one. The church alive deals with a world alive, and this demands leaders with differing gifts and methods, which in turn means differences of appeal and effectiveness and influence.

3. Humility becomes us because *our physical presence and natural powers are limited.* The apostle Paul admitted his own limitations in this

area, if our usual reading of 2 Corinthians 10:10 is correct: "For they say,"—was this a reference to a formal charge voiced by some whom Paul had failed to win?—" 'His letters are weighty and strong, but his bodily presence is weak, and his speech contemptible.' " If this was an actual complaint and not Paul's use of literary diatribe to make a point, it indicates those critics' lack of esteem for Paul's personal presence and scorn for his traits as a speaker.[12] Were some of Paul's opponents so crass as to plague him with publicly stated insults like those about his physical appearance? Did they scorn him because of visible defects, from some eye disease, or malaria, or epilepsy perhaps, or from several beatings suffered or having been stoned (2 Cor. 11:24–25)? Whatever his physical problems were, Paul had learned to live with them and to do his work in spite of them. As we live, labor, and age, we too will know not only physical benefits but physical problems, and the way we handle our problems can often influence the way people view and regard us. Scotsman James Macgregor had a boyhood plagued by having to face the public; he was reticent to be in public because he had short, twisted, and deformed legs. After being called into ministry Macgregor thought that his physical circumstance would confine him to some out-of-the-way place of service, fearing that his bodily appearance would be reprehensible to parishioners. But despite that, he went on to fame as a beloved pastor for forty years at St. Cuthbert, a large and outstanding church.[13] Macgregor discovered that spiritual endowment can outrank and overshadow physical limitations. James Morison (1816–93), of Glasgow fame, also learned this. After suffering an injury in his vocal cords, Morison's voice was low and coarse and generally weak, although at times, while he was speaking, his larynx became heated and his voice seemed closer to the old and desired sound.[14] Although his tone was not as orchestrated as before, Morison remained encouraged and kept his speech attractive and his content rich. He made sure that when his hearers had to strain to hear him, it would be worth their effort to listen and his to speak. Robert W. Dale (1829–95), the noted English Congregationalist and the first Englishman to give the Beecher Lectures at Yale (1877), suffered from a periodic nervousness and had times of inward struggle with emotional depression. His problem was rooted in the temperament he had by nature. Later, in his old age, when his assistant George Barber was undergoing a similar kind of emotional strain, Dale advised him, "Give God thanks for your temperament."[15] Dale was advising out of his own sad experience of a nervous collapse that had laid him aside for three months. Just into his thirties, he had become sole pastor at the Carr's Lane Church in Birmingham, England, when senior pastor John Angell James died in 1859 after but a few hours' illness; young Dale had been James's associate for six years.[16] The experience of that "down time" mellowed R. W. Dale for a meaningful ministry, but he had to watch himself with great care across the rest of his years.

Englishman Frederick William Robertson (1816–53), the now-celebrated Brighton preacher, was equipped with a ready genius, handsome looks, and an intense devotion to his calling, but he suffered from a highly sensitive nervous system that caused him to be intensely inward and outwardly distant at times. Near the end of what proved to be a short life, Robertson's languor and dark moods deepened because of increasingly severe head pains; only later was it discovered that these were the result of an abscess that had developed at the base of his brain. Interestingly, Robertson recorded some brief notes about what he was experiencing from his malady. One of those notes, penned just a few days before he died, ended as a scratchy, incomplete attempt, its lines zigzagged because written in extreme pain: "I shall not get over this. His will be done! I write in torture." That word, "torture," was the last word Frederick William Robertson ever wrote. But in an earlier letter during that time of distress, Robertson had written to one of his minister friends: "It is a wise man's duty to try to work within his limitations in the best way he can, and grumble as little as possible: or else cut himself asunder at once from all restrictions and obligations, by giving up his sphere of work entirely."[17] There are times when we face physical limitations that cannot be overlooked as we seek to fulfill our stewardship, but divine grace for dealing with them can always be our portion, assuring a wonderful triumph of mind and spirit over matter.

John Hall (1829–98) voiced this wise word, among many others, when giving his Beecher Lectures at Yale in 1874: "Physical conditions are not despicable, as many a feeble-bodied preacher knows. You cannot determine the strength of your chests, or the vigor of your constitutions; but you can conserve what you have received, by proper food, little enough of it, pure air, and sufficient exercise."[18] We who preach must work with what we each have been given. We are not all equally endowed intellectually or physically, and we must learn how wisely to relate our given equipment to the demands of our given task. Charles Sylvester Home (1865–1915), a magnetic and supremely gifted preacher who gave the Beecher Lectures at Yale in 1914, died one year later, but forty-nine years old, and probably, W. Robertson Nicoll commented, because "he could not measure the limits of his strength or unfailingly keep within them. It was his nature to answer every call, and to encumber himself with labour that was for others rather than for him."[19]

4. Humility is our needed attitude because *our knowledge is limited.* Like Paul, we should be honest and humble enough to admit that "we know only in part" (1 Cor. 13:9a). However studious, learned, and avid in thought, we each know all too little. What we do know can often be enough for God's use at a given time, provided we humbly use it to God's glory and not our own.

5. Humility should mark our lives because *our time for living and serving is limited.* That is a reality. Your steps and mine are marked, and our days are numbered. Despite the greatness of our task and the strategic importance of any assignment—and what is of higher value than speaking for God?—the time will come when we each will be forced by life to "let go" and die, leaving some assignment unmet, some duty unfinished, some dream unfulfilled. As Henry Wadsworth Longfellow so ably voiced it,

> Labor with what zeal we will,
>   Something still remains undone,
> Something uncompleted still
>   Waits the rising of the sun.[20]

Yes, the time comes for each and all to "let go" and die. To be sure, we will die even if there is no willingness to "let go."

"Something uncompleted" remained when Vernon Johns (1892–1963), Martin Luther King Jr.'s legendary predecessor at Dexter Avenue Baptist Church in Montgomery, Alabama, collapsed, dead, after his speech at Howard University, uncannily, on "The Romance of Death."[21] "Something uncompleted" remained when Sandy F. Ray (1898–1979), another eminent Baptist preacher and friend, died in

1979 while in his Cornerstone Baptist Church pulpit in Brooklyn, New York. "Something uncompleted" remained when the supremely gifted and stupendously gracious Samuel DeWitt Proctor (1921–97), one of America's most respected preachers and educators, and a treasured friend, died in May 1997 in Cedar Rapids, Iowa, following a heart attack; although long since "retired," and still mindful of a long-term heart condition, he was in Iowa lecturing, still eager to help faith grow in hard places, still busy being a steward for God, eager to preach and influence others to fulfill their God-given potential. He had been in university and church work for fifty years but still had some important items on his agenda that he thought could bring the formal assignments of his career to a climax. Mindful in 1989 of physical uncertainties he faced as he retired, yet eager about his stewardship duties, Samuel Proctor stated with great moral resolve: "I will use all of my time left, God willing, to preach the gospel of Jesus Christ and to advocate the pursuit of real community in America and in the world."[22]

We come into this world and live for a time. We find our work after a time and do our work for a time. Then, in spite of the importance of that work and the successes or disappointments related to it all, we must in time leave it all. That is a reality. And that reality underscores the ultimate importance of The Story entrusted to our telling, for The Story promises and points to the reality of a life beyond this one, and to rewards for faith and faithfulness during our life here. Hear anew that cheering promise our Lord made: "Be faithful until death, and I will give you the crown of life" (Rev. 2:10b). And anticipate, with eager me, being the one fondly addressed by our Lord in these words: "Well done, thou good and faithful servant: thou hast been faithful over a few things, I will make thee ruler over many things: enter thou into the joy of thy lord" (Matt. 25:21 KJV). These are promised realities to crown that new and eternal estate of every true believer and every faithful steward of God.

> To serve the present age,
> My calling to fulfill,
> O may it all my pow'rs engage
> To do my Master's will.[23]

6

The Gracious Imperative

A Sermon on Mark 1:16–20

"As Jesus passed along the Sea of Galilee, he saw Simon and his brother Andrew casting a net into the sea—for they were fishermen. And Jesus said to them, 'Follow me and I will make you fish for people.' And immediately they left their nets and followed him. As he went a little farther, he saw James son of Zebedee and his broher John, who were in their boat mending the nets. Immediately he called them; and they left their father Zebedee in the boat with the hired men, and followed him."

I

Four hallowed names rise up like mountain peaks within this text: Simon, Andrew, James, John, four persons Jesus brought together and kept related across the rest of their lives by his purpose and planning. What a treasured account this is!

Simon, Andrew, James, and John: What honored names in Christian history! In reading Mark's all-too-brief report about these four, one wishes for more details about that crucial meeting when they heard and answered Jesus' call to follow and remain with him. As they later ministered, introducing themselves to changing audiences and sharing their message in the midst of changing times, what a time of deep

51

drama it must have been to hear any one of them tell what it felt like to become an intimate with Jesus. We all know the later history of these four men, but the story of those great happenings later in their lives only makes this brief account of how their discipleship began all the more attractive, and all the more engaging.

Clive Sansom, a British poet, was sensing the drama that fills this account when he imaginatively put himself in Andrew's shoes:

> . . . the water lay calm, unrippled,
> And no wind blew. . . .
> It was then, with his own peace, he came.
> Simon and I were casting together,
> Thigh-deep in the liquid sunset.
> Herod's barge had passed in the distance.
> Whirling my weighted net about my head
> I watched it fall, open and spread
> Like the skirts of a dancer.
> As it sank to the lake-floor
> I pulled the cord and, the mouth closing,
> Was dragging it beachward. . . . There he stood—
> Smiling seriously at our surprise—
> Jesus—last seen with the Baptist.
> Our dropped nets bulged on the pebbles.
> "Come with me. . . . You will fish for [people]."[1]

David S. Bell, who has spent several years in ministry to youth, told of using this Bible passage at camps and youth retreats and asking young people to list all the possibilities they can for why Simon, Andrew, James, and John left their boats—and their careers—to follow Jesus. One of the first answers was a typical teenager's response: they left their boats and went off with Jesus because they were bored with what they had been doing; they knew that they could always return to their fishing business. Another answer was that they were attracted to Jesus because of his growing popularity among the people; perhaps their own ambition to be recognized leaders moved them to become associated with him. A third answer carries us deeper: perhaps they were prodded by God's Spirit to trust and follow him—"they just knew from within that this was a call from God, which they didn't fully recognize until much later in life."[2]

Some years ago, while preaching at a Christian college about discipleship, I referred to the response these four men made to the call of Jesus upon their lives. Not long afterward I received an envelope from one of the English professors who had heard that sermon; in the envelope was a newly crafted poem the professor had imaginatively written about the emotion seething within Zebedee as he watched James and John, his sons, trailing off with Jesus, having left him, the work scene, and the family business. The professor captioned the poem "Zebedee's Complaint":

> Along came that man, and without any warning,
> He ordered my sons (as if he had the right!)
> To get out of the boat, where we mended our fishnets,
> And go with him, with little regard for my plight.
> I've labored for many years, building this business,
> And it's yielded a living—all a father could wish.
> But I did it for *them*, planned it all for *their* future,
> Taught them all of my skills. (People always need fish!)
>
> He didn't consult me, this vagabond preacher.
> It was I who begot them, and made of them men
> To be proud of—responsible. Then in an eye-blink
> He spoke, and they turned into children again.
>
> His words had a note of finality. Clearly
> No idle whim prompted his "Come, follow me."
> For what foolishness have they abandoned their duties?
> Will they ever come back to their life on the sea?
>
> Oh, it hurts! I would not have believed they could do it—
> In a trice, all my plans for their future erased.
> They have scorned their inheritance, left all to follow
> In the footsteps of one plainly mad. What a waste!

Whatever Zebedee's emotional response might have been, we know what his sons did: they answered the call of Jesus with openness to the purpose behind and within that call. His promise made them believe that Jesus envisioned something meaningful for them. Together with Simon and Andrew, they obediently "followed" Jesus and became what he promised to make them become.

Guided by this text, let us trace anew what it means to "follow" Jesus, and how following him readies us to live and labor with a sense of high purpose.

II

"Following" Jesus, also known as Christian discipleship, begins with an experience that associates us with Jesus. The ministry of Jesus was filled with the activity of meeting people, "calling" them into fellowship with himself. All who heard such a call felt an authority—a winsome, trust-inviting, and life-engaging authority.

Every call Jesus issued was uttered with graciousness. He spoke imperatively, yes, but every imperative was graciously issued, and what he asked bore the marks of inspiration and the distinct challenge of a high purpose. Every call Jesus issued grew out of his vision for the person he addressed; it made each respondent a candidate for a purposeful life. We see proof of this in what happened to Simon, Andrew, James, and John.

There is in the Mishnah, in the "Benedictions" (Berakoth) section of that treasured compilation of Jewish oral tradition about the Law, a passage in which a rabbi explained what it means to respond positively to God's word as one who hears it. According to that rabbi, to "hear" truly is to take on the yoke of the kingdom of heaven; it is to willingly subject oneself to divine sovereignty and to let God fully order one's life.[3] Jesus used that same image of the yoke when he invitingly said: "Take my yoke upon you, and learn from me" (Matt. 11:29a).[4] Stating the matter of obedience to God as taking on a yoke was common in Judaism, but in this invitation Jesus had more in mind than helping someone become a better student of the Law. What Jesus said meant more because he spoke and speaks as God's calling Agent. He summoned hearers to yield their consent to God. This is what Jesus was asking of Simon, Andrew, James, and John when he issued that gracious imperative, "Follow me." This is what Jesus asks when he addresses us with his inviting word today.

III

The promise of Jesus to those four was that in following him they would *become* "fishers for people." Obedience in following, openness to learn, and loyalty to him were all that Jesus required to make them what he envisioned they could become.

Jesus had in mind a ministry for those four, a specialized service in his name. That ministry could not begin until they were made ready for it, and the promise of Jesus was that he would "make" them ready.

Ardent disciples do not seek their own ends, and effective ministers are never self-made. The Lord must be our central teacher, and only he can rightly prepare those who are to serve God's special interests. That preparation begins with being a "disciple," a learner at the feet of the Master. The educational systems of our time do not even hint at what this way of learning meant in that earlier day. In our time, students are concerned with learning facts, acquiring knowledge, completing prescribed courses, and getting distinguished grades, but in the time of Jesus, the teacher-student relationship had to do with learning a way of life. It involved a learning process that shaped a person's character and determined that person's future. The aim of the teacher was to implant learning, yes, but a learning that would imprint the character of the teacher upon the student's life. That is the blessing that Simon, Andrew, James, and John received and honored, and for which we honor their names. They accepted the plan of Jesus for their lives. The tragedy of Judas was that he resisted the Master's plan, filled with notions, motives, and a vision of his own. Trying to maintain control over his own life, make his own way, and earn his own place, Judas fell into ruin.

Simon (Peter), anxious to save himself when he felt threatened, later lapsed in discipleship and failed the Lord's trust of him by a string of selfish lies. You remember the incident. How gracious Jesus was when he confronted Simon after that failure! He restored that chastened and repentant man to a place of intimacy as a disciple and summoned him anew to the original task. Using the same words of call spoken earlier at the seaside, Jesus bade him, "Follow me" (John 21:19b). Following Jesus has always meant obeying him, staying open to learn from him, and this happens when there is a loyalty to him that is rooted in gratitude and love.

Simon, Andrew, James, and John had special assignments awaiting them in the future. They would be sent to "fish" for people. This would demand an interest in people. Following Jesus finally readied those four to move effectively among people, armed with a God-inspired interest to help them. That is what any ministry is all about. All are called to "follow" Jesus, to be disciples of the Master and show the imprint of his character upon our lives, but some are destined for special ministries in his name in order to serve God's interest among the people. All of us should be willing to leave our "boats and nets" for his sake, but Jesus does not lay that demand upon all. I am reminded of the Gerasene demoniac whom Jesus healed; the delivered man was so grateful to Jesus that he "begged that he might be [remain] with him; but Jesus sent him away, saying, 'Return to your home, and declare how much God has done for you'" (Luke 8:38–39). Not all are called to leave a career and home when touched by the life of Jesus; some must remain at home and share their witness about him there.

IV

And now, one more item of prime concern: do not overlook *the grand partnership those four developed and enjoyed as disciples and ministers* because of Jesus. As Jesus passed by, saw these four, and called them, they were working in teams, aware of a common bond and a common task as they busily worked at the business of their day. This continued and deepened across the rest of their lives, and they were all blessed and enhanced because of it.

Sustained discipleship and creative ministry have always fared best when there has been a caring and responsible partnership among believers. How else could they have handled the multiple demands of "fishing for people"? Partnership strengthens character. Partnership generates trust and encourages openness. Yes, partnership is strategic because it guarantees community and enhances competence. Partnership between believers and those with specialized ministries promotes attentiveness to a shared vision and deepens commitment to an understood task. How else, I ask again, how else can the multiple demands of "fishing for people" be handled?

In speaking about "fishing for people" Jesus meant more than evangelistic efforts that call people to decision but go no further with regard to their lives and needs! Rightly understood, the metaphor about "fishing for people" is a comprehensive symbol that includes all the ministry functions necessary to fulfill kingdom demands and meet human needs.[5] This expressive metaphor is a job description, on the one hand, and a call to unity, on the other. Even though Jesus chose this metaphor because he was addressing fishermen, the point remains the same: if the best is to result as we do an assigned work, then partnership in doing it is a must.

Interestingly, the fishing metaphor Jesus used initially when he called Simon, Andrew, James, and John does not appear with prominence in the later record. Afterward, away from the seaside—which perhaps inspired his use of that metaphor—Jesus spoke of ministry in other ways. He sometimes used pastoral terms, as when, after the resurrection, he instructed Simon Peter, "Feed my sheep" (John 21:17). Earlier, he had highlighted the evangelistic aspect of ministry when he told the disciples that the throngs of people were like "fields . . . ripe for harvesting" (John 4:35). Yes, Jesus described ministry in different ways. In that land of shepherds, he drew on shepherding as an image of the pastoral and nurturing aspects of ministry. In that land of many vineyards and crop-filled fields, he also spoke of sowing seeds and cultivating growth, of reaping, of sheaves and harvest, of gathering fruit and grain, using all these as metaphors of ministry. But whether Jesus' reference was to fishing, sowing and reaping, or leading and tending sheep, a labor was involved for which faithfulness was required, *with partnership*. In laboring as partners, that illustrious company of four did not fail. If we follow Jesus faithfully, we too can succeed!

Daniel S. Warner understood this, and this song of his prods us to that needed industry, diligence, and partnership:

> We will work for Jesus and adore the plan
> That exalteth so a fallen race,
> Joining with the Savior, doing what we can
> To extend the wonders of his grace.
> . . . .
> We will work for Jesus, we are not our own;
> Jesus, we can never idle be;
> Souls around us dying, purchased for thy throne;
> We will gather all we can for thee.
>
> [Let us] work for Jesus,
> [Let us] work for Jesus,
> [Let us] live for him who died for all;
> [Let us] work for Jesus,
> [Let us] work for Jesus,
> Till we hear the final trumpet call.[6]

7

On Being a Leader

A Sermon on Isaiah 55:1–7

Ho, everyone who thirsts,
    come to the waters;
and you that have no money,
    come, buy and eat!
Come, buy wine and milk
    without money and without price.
Why do you spend your money for that which is not bread,
    and your labor for that which does not satisfy?
Listen carefully to me, and eat what is good,
    and delight yourselves in rich food.
Incline your ear, and come to me;
    listen, so that you may live.
I will make with you an everlasting covenant,
    my steadfast, sure love for David.
See, I made him a witness to the peoples,
    a leader and commander for the peoples.
See, you shall call nations that you do not know,
    and nations that do not know you shall run to you,
because of the LORD your God, the Holy One of Israel,
    for he has glorified you.

Seek the LORD while he may be found,
    call upon him while he is near;
let the wicked forsake their way,

and the unrighteous their thoughts;
let them return to the LORD, that he may have mercy on them,
and to our God, for he will abundantly pardon.

Verse 55:4 refers to David, who is mentioned by name in the preceding verse. David was the Hebrew nation's second king, the regal ruler who founded the long-lasting dynasty that ruled in the capital city of Jerusalem. I have selected this text because its wording allows and helps us to review together some features of the kind of leader God shapes, anoints, sends, and uses to accomplish his will among and through his people. Here, again, is that text: "See, I made him a witness to the peoples, a leader and commander for the peoples."

I

It is clear from this text, written several centuries after David's death, that his kingship was still held in honor, and, more so, that the leadership he had modeled was still being regarded as the benchmark for a monarch. By this time in the nation's checkered history, more than twenty from David's bloodline had followed him on the throne, but only two of them—Hezekiah and Josiah—had come close to the model leader David had been; nearly all of the others had been selfish, ungodly monarchs—"political animals," we might well label them— and some had been guilty even of idolatry, which was the worst of sins for a Hebrew.

Godly prophets had done their work of witnessing for God during the reign of those faulty leaders, but generally to no avail. The people continued to stray from the terms of the covenant and therefore from God. The end result was as those prophets warned: God punished the nation by letting the people suffer as captive exiles in Babylon for seventy years.

Our text about David is set within a cluster of prophecies God addressed to the Hebrews during their years in exile. Throughout chapters 40–55, God is heard speaking anew to his people. The word from God was that his promises to their ancestors had not been revoked and that those promises would begin to be fulfilled if his people would return to him. This was the condition the people needed to meet, the requirement long known but, alas, long disregarded. Thus the invitational appeal from God with which chapter 55 begins. God was eager for his people to return to his guidance. God wanted to meet their needs and bless them.

The manner and wording of the appeal are quite striking. The manner is that of a street vendor, eagerly and loudly hawking to the populace, intent to attract interest and gain sales.

> 55: 1a Ho, everyone who thirsts,
>   come to the waters;

But the vendor who speaks in this chapter is different. This street vendor is not seeking a sale but is rather offering to give something away. It is as if at a time of famine, depression, or public need some rich benefactor has sent this vendor forth to distribute freely to those in need what they, lacking money, could not buy:

> 55:1 Ho, everyone who thirsts,
>   come to the waters;
> and you that have no money,
>   come, buy and eat !
> Come, buy wine and milk
>   without money and without price.

And then, almost immediately afterward, the prophet announced the deeper issue within that invitation:

> 55:6 Seek the LORD while he may be found,
>   call upon him while he is near;
> 55:7 let the wicked forsake their way,
>   and the unrighteous their thoughts;
> let them return to the LORD, that he may have mercy upon them,
>   and to our God, for he will abundantly pardon.

The people were being summoned to return to God. God was inviting them back, eager to forgive them and restore the freedom and the place of privilege they lost because of their grievous sins. Thus verse 12, with its welcome promise that their captivity would end and that they would be "led back in peace" to Jerusalem, their homeland.

II

This was a fresh word to the nation, and in it God announced his concern to covenant anew with the people; in fact, the people are told that just as God had used David for a special function in the world, he was willing to use them in a special way as well. Just as David had fulfilled his positive mission to be "a witness to the peoples, a leader and commander for the peoples," God was offering them a future as his servants among the nations. Thus the wording in 55:5:

> 55:5 See, you shall call nations that you do not know,
>   and nations that do not know you shall run to you,
>   because of the LORD your God, the Holy One of Israel,
>   for he has glorified you.

The promise from God, then, was that a truly repentant people would not only receive pardon but be used in a prophetic purpose, as David had been.

That, in brief, is the background to our text. Let us now examine the insights the text offers about leadership.

III

Notice, first, that in speaking about David, the text reports God saying that it was he who readied David for leadership. "I made him," God states. "*I* made him a *witness* [*ʿēd*] to the peoples" (v. 4). Since a witness is someone who can give testimony or evidence from personal knowledge or experience, we should understand that *a personal knowledge about God is strategic and imperative for being a spiritual leader.*

David had an honored name as a witness: He witnessed about the steadfast love of the Lord. He witnessed about the forgiving mercies of the Lord. He witnessed about the delivering power of the Lord. He witnessed about the guidance and providential protection God grants to those who look to him. An unhurried reading of Psalm 18, among others psalms, will show some of David's witness about God and God's dealings with him. Take special notice of 18:30, which tells us that the same God in whom David trusted will prove himself God to all who look to him as David did: "This God—his way is perfect; the promise of the LORD proves true; he is a shield for all who take refuge in him." "I made him a witness," the text states. *A relevant spiritual leader is always someone who can give personal witness regarding God's place and work in their own life.*

Notice, second, that the text reports God's statement that he had appointed David to his position as "a leader [*nagid*] and commander [*tsavah*] for the peoples" (Is. 55:4). Since a leader is one who goes before, guiding, directing those who follow, and since a commander is someone who exercises authority and gives orders to guide a process and achieve an envisioned end for the group, we should understand that *relevant spiritual leadership requires something more than human ambition or even scholarly attainment: it requires divine anointing.*

David's imperial power to lead and command was by God's design, God's trust, and God's anointing. God entrusted the role of kingship to David. And that role was not for David's honor personally but, as the text states, "for [in the interest of] the peoples."

God had sovereign reasons for choosing David, especially since the latter portion of David's story holds some glaring failures, but I would like to name six qualities of David that God knew could be harnessed and used to make him the leader and commander the people needed. The six letters in the word "leader" can be used to show those six qualities.

1. David knew what it meant to be *loyal:* loyal to a heritage, loyal to a people, loyal to granted authority, loyal to trust, loyal to principles, loyal to God.
2. David was an *earnest* person, serious in his intention, zealous in his concerns.
3. David was an *alert* person; he was "fully attentive," wide awake, very aware. Alertness makes a person magnetic and attractive to others. Ralph Waldo Emerson commented in his essay on "Power" that "there are men, who, by their sympathetic attractions, carry nations with them, and lead the activity of the human race."[1] David was such a man.
4. David was a person of *discipline.* He was trained to live and act in accordance with rules and wisdom. He did not shrink from what had to be done when it was painful or problematic to do it. He moved ahead, strengthened and steadied by discipline. There is a sage saying, attributed to Publilius Syrus, "Any one can hold the

helm when the sea is calm." Disciplined persons adapt their effort to the demands they face, and they do so aided by a sense of purpose.

5. David, as you well know, was a man of *empathy*. He had the ability to suffer vicariously with others.

6. David honored *responsibility*. He was willingly and readily accountable for what was placed under his control and management.

Loyalty, earnestness, alertness, discipline, empathy, a sense of responsibility: these six qualities are basic for a sound and stable personality, which, surrendered to God's control, can be enlisted and enhanced by God for his service. The model leader is, after all, a prime example of God's way of dealing with us. That leader is a surrendered self who has gained the wisdom and warmth that follows being obedient. God trains those destined to lead by helping them first learn to follow. Aristotle, in his study on *Politics*, rightly pointed to this need when he wrote that someone who has never learned to obey cannot be a good commander.[2] *The relevant leader is always someone who has learned to follow God's lead and who remains surrendered to God's appointment for their life.* And that appointment is always with the interest of others in view. "See, I made him a witness to the peoples, a leader and commander for the peoples."

IV

I have been speaking about David, Israel's second king, as a revered leader because the text honors him as such. David's name is still remembered and regarded for his exemplary leadership. In the economy of God's plan, David's appointment and accomplishments were afterward viewed as distinctly emblematic of the promised Messiah. We know that Messiah as Jesus of Nazareth, because Scripture tells us that "God has made him both Lord and Messiah" (Acts 2:36).

David's leadership was exemplary in many ways, and we can learn much from his career. But the Ultimately Relevant Leader is our Lord Jesus Christ; he is the Righteous One whose mission we must trust for our salvation. It is to him that we must remain surrendered, and it is he whom we must obediently follow as Messianic Leader and Lord.

The apostle Peter understood this, and out of his experience of being restored after a sad failure he wrote, "For to this you have been called, because Christ also suffered for [us], leaving [us] an example, so that [we] should follow in his steps. 'He committed no sin, and no deceit was found in his mouth.' When he was abused, he did not return abuse; when he suffered, he did not threaten; but he entrusted himself to the one who judges justly. He himself bore our sins in his body on the cross, so that, free from sins, we might live for righteousness" (1 Pet. 2:21–24a). What a Savior! What a model! What a Lord!

The apostle Paul also understood this, and lived it, which is why he could say, "Be ye followers of me, even as I also am of Christ" (1 Cor. 11:1 KJV). What a commitment! What an example! What an appeal!

8

This Jesus

A Sermon on Hebrews 13:8

"Jesus Christ is the same yesterday and today and forever."

"If [people] have pondered the mystery of themselves, they have even more contemplated the mystery of Jesus . . . yet not all have understood him thoroughly, and their conclusions about him have been diverse."[1] So wrote one of my seminary professors, Thomas S. Kepler, now deceased, a saintly believer who had not only a well-stocked mind but a godly, contagious spirit. Kepler made that comment more than sixty years ago in introducing his anthology *Contemporary Thinking about Jesus.* Then, as now, an insatiably news-hungry public was showing interest in what thinkers were saying and writing about Jesus. A new generation of thinkers is now at work publishing their assessments, and the surge of publications about Jesus of Nazareth has even captured media attention, deepening public interest in this subject area. I do not stand here to review the continuing debate about Jesus. I rather stand here as a spokesperson for the One about whom the debate rages, and I use a text that links him signally to our faith, our proper future, and our desired fulfillment. It is a text that can help us understand Jesus adequately for a confident trust, a loyal discipleship, and a faithful service in his name. I mention understanding Jesus "adequately" because in confronting the New Testament truths regarding Jesus our faith must forever seek understanding, since to meet him is to experience mystery. The writer of Hebrews knew this, so he wrote to explicate and emphasize anew what Jesus means for believers: "Jesus Christ is the same yesterday and today and forever." Part of the writer's summarizing word in a well-written epistle, this text holds before us a majestic conclusion for the faith that saves, satisfies, and sustains. "Jesus Christ is the same yesterday and today and forever."

I

In light of all that precedes in the epistle, the writer means that *this Jesus is utterly distinctive in the plan of God to meet our deepest human need*. This is why he is referred to here as "Jesus *Christ.*" The title "Christ" is central for understanding *this* Jesus adequately, since he alone was ordained by God as the anointed One for humankind.

The personal name "Jesus" (the Greek form of the Hebrew "Joshua") was somewhat popular and common among Jews down through the centuries before the common era. Scattered references in the works of Josephus list several contemporaries of Jesus who held the same personal name, and because this was so, Josephus carefully distinguished between them by making some necessary comments about each one.[2] One Jesus served as high priest during a part of the Maccabean period, succeeding his dead brother Onias. Strongly influenced by Hellenistic culture, he promoted Greek customs and even changed his name to Jason, a Greek name. Second Maccabees 4 refers to him as ambitious, ungodly, and vile. He was not like *our* Jesus. Another Jesus, son of See, also a high priest, served a few years before Annas was appointed. Yet another Jesus, son of Damnios, also a high priest, served about AD 62–63. There was also Jesus, son of Gamaliel, who served as high priest AD 63–65. Later, still another Jesus, son of Sapphias, became high priest. All these men bore the name Jesus. Each one was noticed in life, and some were in some respects notable, but not one of them was like *our* Jesus. Only Jesus of Nazareth bore and bears the title "Christ."

As a common name, Jesus was no longer used by Jews after the second century, since most were opposers of the church. And Christians would not use it for their children because the name was too hallowed for any except Jesus of Nazareth to wear. A once-common name thus became restricted, being either rejected by unbelievers or viewed as crucial by members of the faith. Jesus Christ holds an utterly distinctive place in the plan of God for humankind. It is a distinction that remains valid "yesterday and today and forever." By divine appointment *this* Jesus holds an unequalled greatness.

He is unequalled, yes, but not unchallenged. One German publication fostered by German Nazis during Hitler's rise to power in Germany stated—in an attitude of audacious sacrilege—"In the centuries to come it will be said by those who look back: 'Christ was great, Adolf Hitler was greater.' "[3] What folly! God used the processes of history to crush both Hitler and his wild claims. General Jodl's remark at the Nuremberg trial about the dead Hitler explains that megalomaniac's greatness: "He was a great man, but an infernal great man."[4] Hitler's life bore the signs of Satan—lying and murder, with a crass disregard for the divine. Hitler himself, a one-time church member, boasted that his path to "greatness" began when he freed himself from the teachings of the church; he claimed that those teachings fenced him in, saying, "I, too, once had that fence around my soul, but I broke it, stick by stick."[5] What Hitler thought was the way to freedom was really the path to destruction. "There is a way that seems right to a person, but its end is the way to death," says the proverb (14:12).

II

Viewed against the background of this epistle, our text reminds us also that *this Jesus is unequivocally divine.* The teachings in this epistle discuss not only the name of Jesus but also his nature.

From the very first sentence in the epistle the writer was eager to declare this truth about our Lord. He began in earnest, using a rich level of rhetoric; the nature of his facts demanded this. He had an emphasis to make, he had some essentials to enumerate, he had some truths to proclaim anew. The divinity of Jesus was one of those truths. Thus this word about our Jesus: "He is the reflection of God's glory and the exact imprint of God's very being, and he sustains all things by his powerful word" (1:3). And hear this: "Let all God's angels worship him" (1:6b). And don't overlook this statement: "Your throne, O God, is forever and ever" (1:8a). Nor this word, "In the beginning, Lord, you founded the earth, and the heavens are the work of your hands" (1:10). And what about this additional statement: "your years will never end" (1:12b). Still other texts in this epistle support the writer's declaration about the divinity of Jesus, but enough has been stated to remind us about this truth that has been described as "one of the unborrowed truths of Christianity."[6] Some believers might suggest that this is also Christianity's most unique truth.

III

The text reminds us as well that *this Jesus is unavoidably decisive for our personal human destiny.* This truth, stated and restated throughout this epistle, forms the very central message of the entire New Testament. From the very first book, the New Testament makes this assertion, presents pertinent facts to support it, and seeks to elicit faith for a relationship with this Jesus. The Christologies the apostles and writers have given us show that one thing was clearly common among them: that this Jesus is God's decisive agent in the world. Daniel T. Niles rightly commented that "the Christian faith is more than a Jesus religion. It is concerned with the consequence to [people] of who Jesus is."[7]

The message elaborated in the New Testament deals with the need for people to know that consequence, act on it, and progressively announce it until the rest of the world has heard it. All who read the Gospels have access to the history on which the message is based and the reason for his coming among us. There is nothing through which anyone must "break" to gain the open facts: this Jesus was born into a Jewish family (Luke 2:1–7); his legal father was one Joseph, a carpenter (Matt. 13:54–56); the family included brothers and sisters (Mark 6:30); although Jesus was doubtless an adept carpenter himself, his major activities were different after he reached thirty years of age (Luke 3:23); he traveled up and down in Palestine preaching, teaching, and healing, talking about the will and ways of God; he trained a group of chosen disciples to do the same (Mark 3:14–15); as he did his work, he became a point of controversy and conflict, accused by the religious leaders of his nation of being a troublemaker and a political menace, which finally led to his death (Luke 23:13–25). This is but a rather hasty sketch of the historical facts. But there is more to the story than this.

The Gospels tell us that God was at work in this Jesus, and in an utterly unique way. The epistles repeat this claim, and so does the book of Acts, which reports how the disciples Jesus trained continued his ministry, effecting results through the authority of his name. Here is a signal statement about this Jesus from one of Peter's heart-searching sermons preserved in the Acts: "There is salvation in no one else, for there is no other name under heaven given among mortals by which we must be saved" (4:12). Paul underscored this in his declaration that "God also highly exalted him and gave him the name that is above every name, so that at the name of Jesus every knee should bend, in heaven and on earth and under the earth, and every tongue should confess that Jesus Christ is Lord, to the glory of God the Father" (Phil. 2:9–11). The statement about his name now being "above every [other] name" amplifies what is meant in saying that he has been exalted; it tells us that Jesus now holds a new rank of decisive and universal dominion, that this Jesus, raised from death, holds divine appointment as both official and essential Lord over all.[8]

IV

Our text has spoken about Jesus as "the same yesterday and today and forever" because time poses no problem to his being or his mission. Time cannot rob us of his work on our behalf; it cannot cheat us out of the benefits he came to give. Time confines us, and by a fatal death stroke it will finally cancel out our names from among the living. Everything that comes to life goes by way of death. Jesus also died, but it is historical fact that he also returned, resurrected, and he continues to minister "through the power of an indestructible life" (Heb. 7:16). Time has not changed the person he is, nor the position he holds. "Consequently he is able for all time to save those who approach God through him, since he always lives to make intercession for them" (Heb. 7:25). Time will take us away, but time will not rob us of the relationship Jesus has made possible for us with God; nor will time cheat us out of knowing him as he is. This Jesus is no figure lost in the past. He does not live by being remembered; he lives because *he is*. This Jesus helps us apprehend God historically, and those who put their trust in him find that he apprehends our personal histories redemptively. Those whom he claims inevitably have no need to try to recapture him.

Controversies over Jesus will continue, and questions about him will continue to be asked. But beyond the questions and the controversies this Jesus still stands—utterly distinctive in the plan of God for humankind, unequivocally divine in nature, and unavoidably decisive for everyone's personal human destiny.

The New Testament message about Jesus remains the same because his person and work remain the same. Thus the text: "Jesus Christ is the same yesterday and today and forever." And thus the writer's warning that follows the text: "Do not be carried away by all kinds of strange teachings" (Heb. 13:9a). "Through him, then, let us continually offer a sacrifice of praise to God, that is, the fruit of lips that confess his name" (Heb. 13:15).

9

On Being Responsible

A Sermon on Hebrews 11:24–26

> "By faith Moses, when he was grown up, refused to be
> called a son of Pharaoh's daughter, choosing rather to share
> ill-treatment with the people of God than to enjoy the
> fleeting pleasures of sin. He considered abuse suffered for
> the Christ to be greater wealth than the treasures of Egypt,
> for he was looking ahead to the reward."

There are some inexorable times in our lives when we must make a personal decision that we know will affect us totally and even determine the course of our future. Those are times when an independent and informed choice is demanded, and we must be personally responsible—and act. Moses was facing such a time in his life. His exact age at that time is not given, but he had "grown up," the text reports. Moses was at that stage in his life where his age, his circumstances, and his awareness had converged to make a decisive choice necessary concerning his future. It was a crucial time. He knew that he would have to go in one direction or another. So: crowded by circumstance he pondered his options; compelled by conviction, he acted responsibly and decided his future.

The account is highly abbreviated. It has that "laconic terseness" that novelist Thomas Mann used to lament when reading about the dimensioned drama in the biblical stories. As a novelist, Mann always wished he could know each biblical story "as life first told it."[1] Despite the abbreviation and compression of the record, our text commends the choice Moses made and reports the grand outcome of that choice. Although "laconically terse," this account offers us needed wisdom about how to be responsible before God.

I

Having "grown up," Moses *acted responsibly by embracing the full facts about himself.* Armed with the knowledge that he was a Hebrew, Moses dropped that designation under which he had lived since a child, "son of Pharaoh's daughter."

Something deep within Moses stirred him to do this. Who would disavow privilege and power for cheap reasons? Moses had known a granted status, the result of having been claimed for life by Pharaoh's daughter, a kind benefactress. As her adopted son, Moses had the benefits of Egyptian culture and learning—and even the possibility of becoming a pharaoh. Moses must have known that Egypt had been ruled and governed by non-Egyptian pharaohs and advisors before, so he must have been mightily stirred from within when, having now grown up, he willfully refused to claim that granted heritage any longer.

My wife Gwendolyn and I were serving under appointment in Jamaica in 1966 when two royal figures visited that nation. One of them was Her Royal Highness Queen Elizabeth of England. The visit of the queen was marked by quiet dignity during the public gathering and a state reception. But one month later, a king visited that island nation—a black, diminutive, elderly king from Ethiopia, Emperor Haile Selassie I. His visit became an event of tremendous public drama. I shall never forget the resounding shout from the black populace when that king emerged from his airplane. Stirred emotion in a jubilant mass of black men, two thousand strong, released itself in that pride-filled shout honoring the black head of one of the most ancient empires in history, and someone with whom they felt a ready identity. It was a deafening roar of welcome accompanied by a virtual forest of palm leaves being waved in his honor. It was a welcome "fit for a king." People do special things for royalty, and a responsible royalty can do significant things for people. It took something special working deep within Moses to persuade him to forfeit the possibility of possessing and using the powers of a king. That special something surely included a deep appreciation of his Hebrew heritage. Continuing to be regarded as "son of Pharaoh's daughter" would not have honored the truth Moses knew about himself. He chose to embrace and declare the full facts about himself, mindful of the cost involved in doing so.

Nursed by his own mother, as we know from the account in Exodus, Moses was doubtless informed and influenced by her. Thus he knew his "Hebrew fact," as we might term it. Had learning Hebrew distinctives made Moses abhor the divinity myths honoring the pharaonic order? Had the brutal slavery system over which pharaoh had full command repulsed Moses' sense of justice and order? Was his decision based on the need to part company with any style of life that allowed and fed upon the misuse of power?

The text tells us that Moses responsibly honored his "Hebrew fact" and refused to live any longer as "son of Pharaoh's daughter." Perhaps he had met some criticisms and slander from those at court who also knew that he was a Hebrew. The Egyptian priests who knew this would certainly act to prevent his rise to power, but Moses was safe because he bore favoring protection as "son of Pharaoh's daughter." As for being disdained by certain priests, Josephus preserved a legend about this. Pharaoh's daughter brought the infant Moses to court one day, and Pharaoh took the boy and held him affectionately to his breast. To please his daughter, Pharaoh took his diadem and placed it on the child's head. When the child playfully knocked the crown off, and it fell to the ground, the watching priests interpreted the action as an omen of ill against the throne of Egypt.[2] Legends aside, we do know that Moses thoughtfully set aside his title of adopted son and thus closed the door to a life planned for him by his benefactress. He felt in his heart what his life must affirm and what he had to reject. His eyes set, his energies focused, Moses took his stand, honoring his convictions.

II

The text tells us that *this responsible action of Moses was decided and accomplished "by faith."* Moses acted in a calculated risk. He projected his future on the basis of a sensed meaning, persuaded by a moment of truth.

Moses was acting responsibly because he let himself be persuaded by the truth. Søren Kierkegaard wisely declared that "the truth is a snare: you cannot have it, without being caught. You cannot have the truth in such a way that you catch it, but only in such a way that it catches you."[3] Moses could not remain in the old life, comfortably settled there, once the truth about himself and his true people seized his heart. Informed by the truth, Moses let himself be influenced by it as well. Instead of feeling undone, he felt undergirded, ready to risk his future, ready to be responsible.

III

Responsible for what? The shape of his future! Responsible to whom? God! That God whose prior action had provided the meanings Moses sensed as imperative for his life.

No word is more central for self-understanding and fulfillment than this one: responsibility. We were envisioned and created to be responsible persons, persons aware of options, but who act with accountability to the truth. This is what Moses did. By following the course truth laid out before him, there was an inevitable connection between his future and the Christ God promised to send. "He considered abuse suffered for the Christ to be greater wealth than the treasures of Egypt, for he was looking ahead to the reward."

The person of faith wisely looks ahead, because faith grants an anticipating and connecting link with the future. If Moses had nostalgically looked back, he might have lamented his losses. If he had selfishly looked around, he would have stooped and staggered under the weight of abuse he received. His decision to forgo the patronage of Pharaoh's daughter meant that he would no longer benefit from granted status and guaranteed protection. He would have to leave Egypt or share in the ill-treatment suffered by the Hebrews, his own people. He had made his decision, and despite the cost, there was no going back.

10

Stay in the Race!

A Sermon on Hebrews 12:1–2

"Therefore, since we are surrounded by so great a cloud of
witnesses, let us also lay aside every weight and the sin that
clings so closely, and let us run with perseverance the race
that is set before us, looking to Jesus the pioneer and perfecter of our faith, who for the sake of the joy that was set
before him endured the cross, disregarding its shame, and
has taken his seat at the right hand of the throne of God."

I

As the time approaches for the international Olympic games to begin,
and as news reports appear regarding athletes who will compete in the
games, I think of many things. I think about how the athletes "psych"
their minds, train their bodies, and set their hopes in preparation to be
winners. I think about former winners, some of whom broke old
records and set new standards by their skill, and about how they
brought their nation, their family, their supporters, and themselves
into prominence by winning. I think about the vow hopeful athletes of
ancient times sometimes made to be victorious and how, when the vow
was fulfilled, a life-size statue of the winner was sometimes prepared
and displayed publicly in that winner's home city.[1] Some of those stat-
ues can be seen in our museums, the athlete's physical development

vividly captured in stone by some sculptor's skills. I think about all this when the time for the new Olympic games approaches.

But I think about more than I have mentioned and about something far more important than gold or bronze medals to be gained. When the time for the Olympic games approaches, I also think about the scene and the summons found in today's text, a text that never fails to stir my spirit to be a winning Christian in the great race of life. The scene is of an athletic event in process, with a great course laid out on which runners are competing before a vast assemblage of concerned observers. The summons is to Christian believers to view themselves as athletes on the race course of life, the successful handling of which demands due preparation, a tested readiness to undergo strain, and a will trained for endurance. Becoming a winning athlete involves this, and so does a successful Christian life.

II

You will have noticed that the text addresses us as athletes, and in the sense I have described, we are. The summons issued in the text is acute, abrupt, deliberate, pointed, and necessary, because we believers sometimes fail to be as serious in Christian concerns as athletes who are eager to win contests. The lack of seriousness shows itself most surely in spiritual unreadiness to handle life's demands. The text mentions "weights" and "clinging sins" as evidences of spiritual unreadiness and strongly urges us to be rid of them.

Athletic readiness has always involved an apt physical development, a well-muscled form, with no flabbiness of flesh. There is in one of the writings of Xenophon the story about Socrates chiding his young colleague Epigenes, who was in poor physical condition. Socrates urged the young man to give himself with seriousness to athletics to build himself bodily. Epigenes replied, "I am not an athlete," meaning perhaps that he had no ambition to have a body bulging with muscles like the professionals. But Socrates would not be put off. The young man's body was in poor order; it lacked strength, zest, and beauty. Socrates asked him what benefit he could be, in that condition, if crisis developed and war came. Then he added that only the fit can save themselves. As for fitness, Socrates went on to mention that fitness comes by labor, it exacts care on one's part, and it never comes of its own accord.[2]

Christian victories also follow fitness and the readiness to endure the stress and strain that challenge the will to win. Spiritual fitness does not come of its own accord; it must be gained, and the text tells us how: "lay aside every weight and the sin that clings so closely, and . . . run with perseverance . . . looking unto Jesus." Every earnest believer will want to understand the rigors of the course and remove all personal obstacles that hinder from within. Whatever it is that burdens personal intent, whatever it is that can hamper our running on for God in freedom, must be laid aside. It should be laid aside willingly, on purpose, and immediately.

As for "the sin that clings so closely," all of us have known some personal and inward things that can be like a trailing garment that entangles our feet, as it were, and trips us—things like selfish, stubborn, sinful attitudes! And nothing can cling closer or trip us faster than an attitude! Mixed motives can also trip us. Serious discipleship requires us to sift our motives, unravel every twisted concern that God points out to us, and center our intent as believers.

A look back at our sinful past will teach each of us about any close-clinging sin we have known. Surely you can remember some wrong to which you were personally drawn before God's grace claimed your life. You can also remember certain weak spots, certain vulnerable places in your life where evil found a somewhat easier entrance into your thoughts and behavior. Yes, all of us can remember where we had obvious problems with ourselves before God graciously provided a delivering solution. Our repentance and initial resolve gave God freedom to forgive us and help us where we needed that deliverance. But we must remain watchful, for it is where we failed before that a spiritual attack against us can seem hardest to handle. The summons in the text is clear, and its counsel is unmistakable: "lay aside every weight and the sin that clings so closely." Some problem that subdued us before can subdue us again, unless we take heed and deepen our resolve to stay in the race.

Two among several spirituals I favor from our black American musical heritage are about resolve, about the will to live for God, honoring one's conviction through to the very last struggle in life. Some of you will recognize this portion from one of them:

> Until I reach my home,
> Until I reach my home,
> I never intend to give the journey over,
> Until I reach my home.

Here are lines from the other one:

> Done made my vow to the Lord
> And I never will turn back.
> I will go, I shall go,
> To see what the end will be.[3]

Notice the emphasis on the "vow," with the Lord as its receiving witness, but the believer has fully accepted the weight of keeping that vow and fully intends to honor it. A struggle with sin and self has taken place, a decision has been made: sinful ways have been abandoned, with a new life to be lived and a worthy goal to be reached at the end. The end of the process is so important that every ounce of one's strength of resolve and endurance will be devoted to reaching that end. That is how intent athletes stay in the race and gain the desired prize. That is also how serious believers deport themselves in the Christian race.

III

Having listened afresh to the summons voiced in the text, let us look more closely now at the stadium scene the text depicts. As we know, the scene is an athletic event in process. The detailed activity is reminiscent of an Olympiad celebration known and regarded in the Mediterranean world since the beginning games in 776 BC at Olympia in Greece. Those early Olympics involved Hellenic athletes from near and far, plus multitudes of supporters and spectators who filled the seats of the stadium. But the stadium also had a special section with seats reserved for veteran winners from previous contests. Those veterans would sit proudly in their seats of honor, and their presence inspired the athletes competing down on the track. Those veteran winners would sit there watching, concerned, prompting, sometimes applauding, each one a figure and symbol of achievement, a living proof of successful endeavor.

Confident that his readers knew about such matters, the writer of the text alluded here to that history in depicting the scene before us. Drawing upon the imagery of a crowded stadium during the Olympics, he sought to encourage some trouble-weary believers to understand themselves as engaged contestants on the great track of life, athletes being watched, prompted, and cheered on by the "great crowd of witnesses" whose faith struggles he had reviewed in chapter 11. "Here you are," he admitted, with pastoral concern. "And there they are!" he suggestively pictured. He seemed to be shouting: "Prophets, priests, and kings are watching you! Warriors, pioneers, fathers and holy women are pulling for you!" The bright-robed witnesses of faith seemed so many as to appear like a great cloud covering the reserved seats in the stadium, each one a hero or heroine of faith, a responsible, sensitive winner, each one a grand soul and achiever, who by example illustrate the awesome strength of faith, the tenacity of perseverance, and the grand dignity of spiritual success, indisputable proof that spiritual preparation and dogged endurance always pay off !

Mind you, the text does not minimize the struggle involved in being a believer; in fact, the text underscores that struggle. It tells us plainly that strain and agony are part of the Christian life. The text faces the facts, and it helps us to face those facts by seeing faces that encourage us to endure them. Living as a Christian is no picnic experience; it is a demanding contest in which we must struggle against evil. The stadium scene in the text, with its pictured host of previous winners, encourages us to expect victory and honor if we comply with its summons and stay in the race.

IV

One afternoon many years ago during a very stressful time in my ministry, a time when my spirit needed a lift, I was standing in the well-decorated sanctuary of the St. Peter and St. Paul Russian Orthodox Church in my home city of Detroit. That church had hosted the monthly meeting of our City Pastors' Union that day, and after the meeting I decided to linger and study the decorative painted scenes filling the sanctuary walls and ceiling. These had captured my interest as our meeting was in progress. The pastor welcomed my questions. He explained that the paintings on the sanctuary walls and ceiling were the work of a refugee artist who had worked across seven years to complete the almost lifelike depictions of faith heroes I stood admiring. I remained a while longer after Pastor Lillikovich left the sanctuary, my mind and heart feasting on the meaning and impact of it all. My studied look at it all made me think about our text, and there deepened in me an understanding of the scene it depicts. I soon felt my heart being "strangely warmed." My thought had moved beyond those painted depictions of apostles and noted Christians from past eras, and I was remembering some grand Christian believers, all deceased, whom I myself had known, all of them stalwart saints. Standing there in that sanctuary that afternoon I experienced a high moment of meaning that still blesses my life, a moment during which remembered faces of known departed saints seemed to appear to me, with eyes focused in my direction, and a message from them seemed to register in my consciousness: "Endure the agony! You can yet win! Stay in the race!" I felt strengthened. I felt encouraged. I felt readied for whatever would be next. Strong emotion fills me now as I report this, and I must confess that it seems almost a sacrilege to speak about it.

In 1981, three years before he died, Dr. Benjamin E. Mays published a second book of autobiographical reminiscences. Many of its pages repeated narratives given before in his majesterial autobiography *Born to Rebel*, but in that second book Mays expanded those narratives by adding more details and included tributes to the many persons in his life who across the years and in many different contexts had, in his words, "driven him on" by their encouragement and help. Dr. Mays took the time to write and name those persons because, as he stated, they "inspired me to do things that I never thought I could accomplish."[4] There are those persons in our world, and some now beyond our world, whose example and experiences are of a quality and force to inspire us and drive us on. That explains why our text pictures for struggling believers that "great cloud of witnesses."

V

Like some of you, I have friends in other church bodies whose liturgy includes a duty to commemorate the righteous dead in prayers and praise, especially on All Saints' Day; a part of the concern is to recognize the church as a beloved community of memory as well as hope. Those of us who are informed by a differing church tradition do not offer prayers for the dead, but we are wise to remember the dead, and we are wiser still if from time to time we express our thanks to God for them, because there are many who, though dead, still bless us by their remembered walk and their worthy work. Our textual passage in Hebrews reflects that Christian writer's regard for the righteous dead. He viewed them as "a cloud of witnesses." They were to him, as they were in fact, ready examples of grand achievements through faith, prime examples of what a tested faith means and can produce.

But while our writer honored the righteous dead as worthy examples, it is not on any of them that he advises us to fix our gaze or set our faith. He directs us to "look to Jesus, the pioneer and perfecter of our faith."

Yes, there is a gathered throng sitting in the upper tier of life. All of those in the throng were good and godly persons through their faith. We each knew some of them. Could we but scan the galleries, penetrating the distance between here and There, we would surely catch sight of a departed friend, a beloved family member, a fellow believer whom we knew well, a pastor, minister, or sainted spiritual advisor who helped us with needed counsel and a trusted care. Could we but see them, their faces no longer hidden from us by the separating mist of death, we would surely see them watching us, showing eagerness for us, pulling for us. If we could not only look but also listen, we would hear them cheering for us.

Holding the center seat among that gathered throng, however, is another figure in that upper tier of life. The writer distinguishes him as Jesus, our Savior, and he tells us to fasten our eyes on him, because Jesus outshines and outranks all others, he being the One who endured the cross and managed its shame redemptively, thus providing for our salvation. No ordeal we experience can match his; no stress we undergo can be as horrid as his; no struggle we face can be more shameful or demanding than his. Look to Jesus! His victory was so exemplary and effective that it remains not only our inspiration but a source of strength.

Look to Jesus! Can you not see him? Concentrate your gaze in faith! Look! Look to Jesus! He is the One with his hand upon his breast, his heart heaving as he watches us run the course. He knows where we are. He understands the strain we feel, and he is sympathetic as we struggle in the race. Look to Jesus! He wants us to succeed, and he steadily prays to God for us. What greater consolation can we find than this? What greater incentive do we need than this? Keep looking to Jesus! Be determined! Gather strength from him, and stay in the race!

11

When Devotion Meets Difficulty

An Easter Sermon on Mark 16:1–6

"When the sabbath was over, Mary Magdalene, and Mary the mother of James, and Salome bought spices, so that they might go and anoint him. And very early on the first day of the week, when the sun had risen, they went to the tomb. They had been saying to one another, 'Who will roll away the stone for us from the entrance to the tomb?' When they looked up, they saw that the stone, which was very large, had already been rolled back. As they entered the tomb, they saw a young man, dressed in a white robe, sitting on the right side; and they were alarmed. But he said to them, 'Do not be alarmed; you are looking for Jesus of Nazareth, who was crucified. He has been raised; he is not here. Look, there is the place they laid him.' "

I

Three duty-minded, devotion-guided women are mentioned in our story, making their way, during an early morning hour, to the tomb where the lifeless body of Jesus had been placed three days earlier. The women are named—Mary Magdalene, Mary the mother of James, and Salome—and they were carrying some fragrant oils they had purchased to use in anointing the body of their Lord. These three were among those who had come up with Jesus from Galilee to Jerusalem when his popularity was at its height; now they moved with sorrowful steps toward the tomb where his crucified body was placed after enemies had succeeded in bringing about his death.

Hasty burial preparations on that awesome Friday had been made, but there was more these women wanted to do. So much had happened so quickly, and his family and friends were all stunned, dismayed, and distressed. Sudden deaths do this to us. Many will remember how our nation was stunned and stupefied when President John F. Kennedy was assassinated. And we were staggered again by the shock received when the news reached us that Martin Luther King Jr. had been killed. And even more recently, when news reached us that Ronald Brown and some American business executives had been killed in a plane crash in Croatia. Sudden deaths shock and affect us, especially the death of persons who mean something to us. The three women in our story had now steadied themselves as best they could, had rallied all remaining strength, and were on their way to anoint the body of Jesus, equipped with fragrant, pungent aromatic oils to pour on the shroud and binding cloths that swaddled it.

Theirs was a deed of honor, not an act of embalming. During the time of Jesus, Jews did not embalm their dead. When someone died, the burial took place, where possible, within twenty-four hours, the haste being required because the heat in that region caused rapid decomposition of the body. In addition, persons who attended the dead person were considered ceremonially unclean, and a swift burial allowed ritual pollution to be dealt with sooner. These women were about to perfume the body of Jesus; they were not trying to preserve it. Thus the "spices" mentioned in the story, those pulverized fragrant substances from which a compound had been prepared and blended with oils so as to saturate the burial wrappings on his body. For those three women this was a way to express devotion for one whose life had meant so much to their own.

II

The devotion these women had for Jesus was something more than a head-thought and a simple heart-feeling. Theirs was a devotion that involved head, heart, hands, and feet. True devotion makes us desire to act, for as John Locke once put it, "Where there is no desire, there will be no industry."[1] Genuine devotion makes us bestir ourselves.

These women were devoted, but as they acted on their devotion, they knew they faced a difficulty: How would they manage the large stone that blocked entrance into the tomb? Each woman knew that there were three of them, and that they were a team, but they also knew that moving the immense stone demanded even more than their combined strength. They had a problem, and they discussed it as they walked, yet they moved steadily toward the tomb. When they arrived, they discovered, to their surprise, that the stone had already been rolled back from the door of the tomb. The difficulty they expected had been handled by Higher Hands! Intent on doing an essential labor, and in the spirit of an authentic love, they were blessed by a divine surprise. In the course of acting out their devotion, those women discovered the surprising activity of God. Like them, we must realize that it is our part to be devoted, while it is God's part to deal with unmanageable barriers in our way. When we are bent on honoring God, on doing service for Jesus, then God delights to act on our behalf and to deal with the heavy stones of difficulty we face, whatever and wherever those difficulties be.

I want to illustrate this, and I begin with an experience from my own life. Many years ago, during my last year at Cass Technical High School, I earned pocket money by serving as pianist for one of our church choirs. I received my stipend on Sunday night after the evening service. A few weeks before the expected June graduation, I went directly from school to the church one Friday afternoon, intent to practice my piano part before the choir rehearsal at church later that evening. After choir rehearsal, I stayed over for the regular Friday night prayer vigil that most of the local ministers of the church attended. The prayer time ended rather late that night, so someone with a car volunteered to drop me along the bus route I knew could get me home without having to change buses, which I usually had to do when not staying in downtown Detroit at my grandmother's.

Once out of my friend's car, standing at the bus stop under the streetlight, I suddenly realized that I had spent so much for lunch that I did not have enough money for my bus fare home. I felt in my pocket and located only four pennies—and a full fare at that time was ten cents! I began praying.

I first prayed that God would let someone drive by who might recognize me and offer a ride. Several cars whizzed by, but no one stopped. I continued praying, and soon remembered the spare nickel I kept stashed away in a secret pocket of my wallet. I opened my wallet and extracted the nickel—grateful for the memory as well as for the forethought to put it away earlier! But I still had only nine cents when I needed ten. I thought of just getting on the bus and taking the risk of asking the driver to let me ride despite my paying less than the full fare, but the thought made me fear being embarrassed, so I dismissed that notion. After all, what would I offer as an excuse to the driver? What driver would have accepted my story?

As I prayed on, aloud, I remembered that I was only a mile or more from a major avenue where a streetcar line offered all-night service in the direction I needed to ride home, so I started walking toward that line. As I got within three blocks of Woodward Avenue, in a section of the block where the streetlight was out, I realized that my foot had kicked a coin. I stopped suddenly, listened intently to the sound of the rolling coin, and went over to where I thought the coin had stopped. I bent over, felt around on the sidewalk in the darkness, soon located the coin, and rushed to the next streetlight to see what I had found. It was a penny! My heart was pounding anxiously as I reached into my pocket to see if perchance I had dropped (and then found) one of the four pennies I knew I had. The other four pennies were still there. I voiced my thanks to God and breathed a sigh of relief. Once at the line, when the streetcar approached, I entered it, sat down, and continued thanking God for answering my prayer. I had needed ten cents to pay my fare, and God had provided the needed penny to complete that amount. I cannot begin to describe the joy I had when that need was met, and that stony fear in my teenage heart of suffering embarrassment was rolled away. That early experience is but one of the many in my life that stir me to report that our God superintends the unmanageable difficulties of those who are devoted to him.

Dr. Samuel DeWitt Proctor was also a gladsome witness about this. In an autobiography published shortly before his sudden and shocking death, Proctor reported that when he was a young student at Virginia

Union an anonymous philanthropist in a New England state paid his tuition. The school never let him know the benefactor's name, perhaps thinking that young Proctor might write not only to thank him but in the brashness of youth respectfully ask for more!

Sixteen years later, Proctor was president of Virginia Union University when a distraught pre-med honor student came to his office with a heavy personal problem. The student was a married veteran with two children, and some circumstances had piled up before him like large, forbidding boulders blocking his path. He was flat broke, his rent was overdue, his children had been sick, and he felt at an end. He already had been accepted into medical school, but saw no way to go on. As Proctor and the student were discussing the matter, his secretary unexpectedly rapped at the door and came into his office. "Sorry to interrupt," she quickly pleaded to the president, "but I think you want to take this call." Feeling the weight of the student's problem, Proctor asked her to tell the person he would have to call them back. "I think you should take it now!" she politely but firmly suggested. He did.

Speaking into the phone, Samuel Proctor heard the cracked, warbly voice of a man ask, "Are you the same Samuel Proctor who went to school at Virginia Union back in 1940?" Proctor answered, "I am the same." "I'm the one who paid your tuition," the man reported. "I called to tell you that I'm satisfied that I made a wise investment. I'm pleased with your progress." Though Proctor was dazed, he managed to utter some words of thanks. But the benefactor was not calling to hear such. He continued, "Can you find me another student that I could help? I don't have much time left, and I would like to do again what I did in your case."

"Sir," President Proctor replied, with the tremor of excitement, "he's sitting in front of me as we speak." Aware that no human could ever align random events with such precision and that God was evidently in this, Proctor handed the phone to the student and left the room. When the student came out of the president's office several minutes later, President Proctor was crying, his secretary was in tears, and the student was smiling through his tears. A forbidding stone had been rolled away. The devotion that brought that student to school and won him a place on the honor roll had stirred him to consult the school's president when circumstances blocked his way. Helped by God, that student, Charles Cummings, became a prominent specialist in internal medicine in Richmond, Virginia.[2]

Stones of difficulty are nothing new to our people, and the awareness that divine help is needed to deal with many of them has been a part of the witness our forebears have left to us. Think of that unyielding stone of slavery that blocked their path as they tried to be true to the same Lord their insensitive masters confessed. As they labored hard in the fields, and often looked with sad eyes up to the big house, they longed for their freedom. Their hope in God had deep roots, and their faith kept them strong, while wisdom told them that "Everybody talkin' 'bout heav'n ain't going there." But always there was that concern: "Who will roll away for us the stone?"

God did! God made possible the steady advance of the Union army, and God superintended the needed emancipation. Slaves from the region rallied in its wake. Once freed, they were going they knew not where, except that the large stone of slavery no longer stood blocking their path. Many songs of deliverance celebrate that freedom, songs like this one:

> Slav-'ry chain done broke at las',
>   broke at las',
>   broke at las',
> Slav-'ry chain done broke at las',
> Goin' to praise God 'til I die.[3]

This song expresses an unmistakable devotion. Like other such spirituals, it reminds us that devotion has its rewards.

There is some unfinished business before us as African Americans, and that business is the right use of our freedom. Our people lived for two centuries under compulsion; now we are free from that compulsion, but many of us lack the commitment that best directs and governs freedom. The anxious longing of our forebears to live without restraints was answered, but as we look across the land, we see those whose liberty has become license and whose unchecked impulses have made problems of dire proportions for us all. Our great need is a properly placed devotion, a devotion centered anew in knowing and serving God. We must guide our people in putting and keeping "first things first." We must help one and all to see that freedom must be directed by a purpose, a high and godly purpose, or we shall be destroyed through lack of one. We humans, all of us, must live by truths, or we will be lost among troubles. We must all be rightly devoted, or we will all be forever mired in difficulties.

III

Well, this ancient story we have reexamined speaks to a contemporary and perennial need—the need to face life's difficulties with realism and a confident courage. This story about those three women is a story of consequence, a story that makes a promise to all who live with their hearts stirred and guided by devotion. Our lives can be bold instead of bankrupt. We can move forward in hope, not backward in hopelessness. The devoted soul lives always with an earnest expectation of good, good given by a concerned God who manages difficulties too immense for our handling. And there is so much in life that we can never manage alone.

But before we leave this story, one more statement must be given: The great deed being reported here is not that the stone blocking the tomb was removed before the women reached it; the great deed this story reports is Jesus' resurrection from death. When the women went into the open tomb, they did not see his corpse, they saw evidence that he was now alive again.

Jesus was raised from death for us. As the apostle reported, "[Jesus] was handed over to death for our trespasses and was raised for our justification" (Rom. 4:25). Death has been dealt with decisively, definitively. This is the message of Easter! The resurrection calls for celebration. Let us rejoice that life's greatest difficulty—the large, hard, mean, and terror-striking fact of death—need not block our path and daunt our hopes. By raising Jesus from death, God has shown us his solution to the most distressing puzzle of our lives. Understanding that this is the case continues to make all the difference in the world to me, and it makes me live differently in the world.

When your devotion meets a difficulty, it is time to trust, not give up, to keep thinking ahead, not turn back. When life tries to shatter your hopes, mire you in the spirit of defeat because of strength-sapping facts, then remember your Savior, assert your soul, declare your faith, and act out your devotion. When your devotion meets difficulty, look at that difficulty in the light of Easter. The Easter event is the key to meaning when you and I are beset by misery. It is the ladder of hope by which to rise up from things that horrify. Easter gives us reason to worship, to celebrate God, as Job did, when things become worse. When your devotion meets with difficulty, remember that God can make the hardest, most stubborn things yield to those who are devoted to him! God himself made death yield to Jesus, and God himself will make difficulties yield to us.

Notes

Preface

1. See *The Responsible Pulpit* (Anderson, IN: Warner Press, 1974); *The Sermon in Perspective: A Study in Communication and Charisma* (Grand Rapids: Baker Book House and Anderson, IN: Warner Press, 1976); *Designing the Sermon: Order and Movement in Preaching* (Nashville: Abingdon Press, 1980); *The Burdensome Joy of Preaching* (Nashville: Abingdon Press, 1998).
2. See *The Responsible Pulpit*, 50, 109; *The Sermon in Perspective*, 52, 54, 75–76; *Designing the Sermon*, 37–38.
3. This analysis is similar to that of Sidney H. Hooke, *Alpha and Omega: A Study in the Pattern of Revelation* (London: James Nisbet & Co., 1961); see esp. 3, 36, 289–91.

Chapter 1: The Preacher as God's Steward

1. On these parables, see Charles H. Dodd, *The Parables of the Kingdom* (New York: Charles Scribner's Sons, 1961); Joachim Jeremias, *The Parables of Jesus* (New York: Charles Scribner's Sons, 1963); for homiletic insights in preaching the parables, see George Arthur Buttrick, *The Parables of Jesus* (New York: Harper & Bros., 1928). See also David Buttrick, *Speaking Parables: A Homiletic Guide* (Louisville, KY: Westminster John Knox Press, 2000).
2. See W. Stephen Gunter, Scott J. Jones, Ted A. Campbell, Rebekah L. Miles, and Randy L. Maddox, *Wesley and the Quadrilateral: Renewing the Conversation* (Nashville: Abingdon Press, 1997). See also Scott J. Jones, *John Wesley's Conception and Use of Scripture* (Nashville: Kingswood Books, 1995).
3. See Gabriel Marcel, *The Mystery of Being*, vol. 2, *Reflection and Mystery*, ed. G. S. Fraser (Chicago: Henry Regnery Co., 1960), esp. 260–61.
4. Gardner C. Taylor, sermon "Jesus Christ," in *The Words of Gardner Taylor*, comp. Edward Taylor (Valley Forge, PA: Judson Press, 2002), esp. 6:120–21.
5. On this passage, see Ralph P. Martin, *Carmen Christi: Philippians 2:5–11 in*

Recent Interpretation and in the Setting of Early Christian Worship, rev. ed. (Grand Rapids: Wm. B. Eerdmans Pub. Co., 1983). See also the discussion of Phil. 2:6–11 in Fred Craddock, *Philippians*, Interpretation: A Bible Commentary for Teaching and Preaching (Atlanta: John Knox Press, 1985).

6. On this, see William F. Orr and James Arthur Walther, *I Corinthians: A New Translation*, Anchor Bible (Garden City, NY: Doubleday & Co., 1976), 177; Anthony C. Thiselton, *The First Epistle to the Corinthians: A Commentary on the Greek Text* (Grand Rapids: Wm. B. Eerdmans Pub. Co., 2000), 335f.

7. Augustine, *De catechizandis rudibus* 2:3, trans. as *The First Catechetical Instruction* by the Rev. Joseph P. Christopher (Westminster, MD: Newman Bookshop, 1946), 15. On Augustine as a preacher, see *The Preaching of Augustine*, ed. Jaroslav Pelikan, trans. Francine Cardman (Philadelphia: Fortress Press, 1973); Peter Brown, *Augustine of Hippo: A Biography*, rev. ed. (Berkeley and Los Angeles: University of California Press, 2000).

8. On this subject, see Bernard Ramm, *Special Revelation and the Word of God* (Grand Rapids: Wm. B. Eerdmans Pub. Co., 1961); Markus Barth, *Conversation with the Bible* (New York: Holt, Rinehart and Winston, 1964); G. C. Berkouwer, *Holy Scripture* (Grand Rapids: Wm. B. Eerdmans Pub. Co., 1975).

Chapter 2: The Steward as Recitalist

1. See Harold C. Schonberg, "Is the Solo Concert an 'Outmoded' Institution?" *New York Times*, September 1, 1974, section D, p. 11; see also Joseph Horowitz, *The Post-Classical Predicament: Essays on Music and Society* (Boston: Northeastern University Press, 1995), esp. 3–13.

2. See the Cooper interview in a sidebar to Robert Rimm's article "The Philadelphia Story," in *Piano and Keyboard Magazine*, January/February 2000, 49.

3. For a fuller discussion of these terms, see Anthony C. Thiselton, "Explain, interpret, tell, etc.," in *The New International Dictionary of New Testament Theology*, ed. Colin Brown (Exeter: Paternoster Press, 1975), 1:573–79.

4. See the documentation and discussion by Gerhard Hasel, *Old Testament Theology: Basic Issues in the Current Debate*, rev. ed. (Grand Rapids: Wm. B. Eerdmans Pub. Co., 1975); see also *Old Testament Interpretation: Past, Present and Future: Essays in Honor of Gene M. Tucker*, ed. James Luther Mays, David L. Petersen, and Kent Harold Richards (Nashville: Abingdon Press, 1995), and *Biblical Theology: Problems and Perspectives; In Honor of J. Christiaan Beker*, ed. Steven J. Kraftchick, Charles D. Myers Jr., and Ben C. Ollenburger (Nashville: Abingdon Press, 1995).

5. Gerhard von Rad, *Old Testament Theology*, trans. D. M. G. Stalker (New York and Evanston: Harper & Row, 1962), 1:121; see also 105–28. For a critical assessment of Gerhard von Rad's theological work on the Old Testament, see D. G. Spriggs, *Two Old Testament Theologies: A Comparative Evaluation of the Contributions of Eichrodt and von Rad to Our Understanding*

of the Nature of Old Testament Theology, Studies in Biblical Theology, Second Series, no. 30 (Naperville, IL: Alec R. Allenson, 1974), esp. 6–10, 34–59. See also Hasel, *Old Testament Theology*, 46–49.

6. G. Ernest Wright, *God Who Acts*, Studies in Biblical Theology, Second Series, no. 8 (London: SCM Press, and Naperville, IL: Alec R. Allenson, 1952).

7. See Walter Brueggemann, *Theology of the Old Testament: Testimony, Dispute, Advocacy* (Minneapolis: Fortress Press, 1997); see also *God in the Fray: A Tribute to Walter Brueggemann*, ed. Tod Linafelt and Timothy K. Beal (Minneapolis: Fortress Press, 1998).

8. See James A. Sanders, *Torah and Canon* (Philadelphia: Fortress Press, 1972), esp. 15–20. Sanders cites 1 Sam. 12:7–9 as the classic summary regarding the saving deeds of God in Israel: "In that one verse the essence of what is recorded in far fuller compass in the Books of Genesis through Joshua is recited" (17).

9. James A. Sanders, *The Old Testament in the Cross* (New York: Harper & Bros., 1961), 14.

10. Elizabeth Achtemeier, *The Old Testament and the Proclamation of the Gospel* (Philadelphia: Westminster Press, 1973), 15. For her elaborations on the problems listed, see esp. 13–44.

11. Amos N. Wilder, *The New Voice: Religion, Literature, Hermeneutics* (New York: Herder & Herder, 1969), 43.

12. On this distinction between historical and history-like, see Hans Frei, *The Eclipse of Biblical Narrative: A Study in Eighteenth and Nineteenth Century Hermeneutics* (New Haven, CT: Yale University Press, 1974), esp. 10–16.

13. James Earl Massey, *Designing the Sermon: Order and Movement in Preaching* (Nashville: Abingdon Press, 1980), esp. 35–49.

14. For more on this, see James Britton, *Language and Learning* (Coral Gables, FL: University of Miami Press, 1970), 191.

15. See Herbert Burhenn, "Religious Beliefs as Pictures," *Journal of the American Academy of Religion* 42, no. 2 (June 1974): 326–35.

16. See Ludwig Wittgenstein, *Lectures and Conversations on Aesthetics, Psychology and Religious Belief*, ed. Cyril Barrett, compiled from notes taken by Y. Smithies, R. Rhees, and J. Taylor (Oxford: Basil Blackwell, 1966); see esp. 53–72.

17. See his "Essay on Experience," in *Ralph Waldo Emerson: Essays and Lectures*, ed. Joel Porte (New York: Library of America, 1983), 472.

18. *Luther's Works*, vol. 26, *Lectures on Galatians, 1535* ed. Jaroslav Pelikan and Walter A. Hansen (St. Louis: Concordia Publishing House, 1963), 199.

19. Francis Wright Beare, *The Earliest Records of Jesus* (Oxford: Basil Blackwell, 1964), 219.

20. Robert C. Tannehill has written a magisterial treatment on this motif in his *Dying and Rising with Christ: A Study in Pauline Theology* (Berlin: Alfred Toepelmann, 1967).

21. See Vincent Taylor, *The Atonement in New Testament Teaching* (London: Epworth Press, 1950); Leon Morns, *The Cross in the New Testament* (Grand

Rapids: Wm. B. Eerdmans Pub. Co., 1965); John Stott, *The Cross of Christ* (Downers Grove, IL: InterVarsity Press, 1987).

22. George Eldon Ladd, *A Theology of the New Testament* (Grand Rapids: Wm. B. Eerdmans Pub. Co., 1974), 413.

23. See Martin Buber, *Die Schrift und ihre Verdeutschung*, with Franz Rosenzweig (Berlin: Schocken Verlag, 1936), 56.

24. Gardner C. Taylor, "Titles," in *Concise Encyclopedia of Preaching*, ed. William H. Willimon and Richard Lischer (Louisville, KY: Westminster John Knox Press, 1995), 492.

25. Phillips Brooks, *Lectures on Preaching* (New York: E. P. Dutton & Co., 1877), 18.

26. Ibid., 18–19.

27. Ibid., 19.

Chapter 3: The Steward and Rhetoric

1. Booker T. Washington, *Up from Slavery: An Autobiography* (Garden City, NY: Doubleday & Co., 1953 reprint of 1900 edition), 244. For a critical study of Washington as a public speaker, see Karl R. Wallace, "Booker T. Washington," in *A History and Criticism of American Public Address*, ed. William Norwood Brigance (New York: Russell & Russell, 1960), 1:407–33.

2. Washington, *Up from Slavery*, 244.

3. Louis R. Harlan, *Booker T. Washington: The Making of a Black Leader, 1856–1901* (New York: Oxford University Press, 1972), 236.

4. On the subject of abstraction as I use it here, see the article in *Dictionary of Philosophy and Psychology*, ed. James Mark Baldwin (New York: Macmillan Co., 1901), 1:6.

5. J. Lindblom, *Prophecy in Ancient Israel* (Oxford: Basil Blackwell, 1962), 152. For an extended treatment of the preaching of the prophets, see esp. 152–65. See also E. W. Heaton, *The Old Testament Prophets* (Baltimore: Penguin Books, 1961); Gerhard von Rad, *Old Testament Theology*, trans. D. M. G. Stalker (New York and Evanston: Harper & Row, 1965), esp. 2:80–95; see also Claus Westermann, *Basic Forms of Prophetic Speech*, trans. Hugh Clayton White (Philadelphia: Westminster Press, 1967), esp. 129–209.

6. See the extensive description by Lindblom, *Prophecy in Ancient Israel*, 155.

7. From among the many studies available on this much-debated issue, see especially Kevin J. Vanhoozer, *Is There Meaning in This Text? The Bible, the Reader, and the Morality of Literary Knowledge* (Grand Rapids: Zondervan Publishing House, 1998), esp. 228–59.

8. See *The Bible in Its Literary Milieu: Contemporary Essays*, ed. Vincent L. Toilers and John R. Maier (Grand Rapids: Wm. B. Eerdmans Pub. Co., 1979); Leland Ryken, *How to Read the Bible as Literature* (Grand Rapids: Zondervan Publishing House, 1984); James L. Bailey and Lyle D. Vander Broek, *Literary Forms in the New Testament: A Handbook* (Louisville, KY: Westminster/John Knox Press, 1992).

9. On these categorical descriptions, see Anders Jeffner, *The Study of Religious Language* (London: SCM Press, 1972), esp. 11–12, 68–104; J. L. Austin, *How to Do Things with Words*, ed. J. O. Urmson (New York: Oxford University Press, Galaxy Book, 1965); John Wilson, *Language and the Pursuit of Truth* (Cambridge: Cambridge University Press, 1960), esp. 47–74.

10. On the relation between the indicative and the imperative in the writings of Paul, see Rudolf Bultmann, *The Theology of the New Testament*, trans. Kendrick Grobel (New York: Charles Scribner's Sons, 1951), 1:332–33, 338–39; Victor Paul Furnish, *Theology and Ethics in Paul* (Nashville: Abingdon Press, 1968), 153–57, 224–27. As for Old Testament instances of the imperative (in law and exhortation, promise, etc.), see James Muilenburg, *The Way of Israel: Biblical Faith and Ethics* (New York: Harper & Row, 1961), esp. 18–30, 74–98.

11. See, for example, Blass, Debrunner, Funk, *A Greek Grammar of the New Testament* (Chicago: University of Chicago Press, 1961), esp. 239–56; A. T. Robertson, *A Grammar of the Greek New Testament in the Light of Historical Research* (Nashville: Broadman Press, 1934), esp. 116–37, 390–445; H. E. Dana and Julius R. Mantey, *A Manual Grammar of the Greek New Testament* (New York: Macmillan Co., 1957), esp. 268–303.

12. James Moffatt called attention to the cumbersome construction, the problematic juxtaposition of clauses and the collocation of separate words, in *An Introduction to the Literature of the New Testament*, International Theological Library (New York: Charles Scribner's Sons, 1915), 387.

13. See Jack T. Sanders, *The New Testament Christological Hymns: Their Historical Religious Background* (Cambridge: Cambridge University Press, 1971), esp. 14–15, 25, 88–92, 97. See also Markus Barth, *Ephesians: Introduction, Translation and Commentary*, Anchor Bible (Garden City, NY: Doubleday & Co., 1974), 1:260–66.

14. Among the many studies of the book of Revelation, see, e.g., Bruce M. Metzger, *Breaking the Code: Understanding the Book of Revelation* (Nashville: Abingdon, 1993); A. W. Wainwright, *Mysterious Apocalypse: Interpreting the Book of Revelation* (Nashville: Abingdon, 1993); and Brian K. Blount, *Can I Get a Witness? Reading Revelation through African American Culture* (Louisville, KY: Westminster John Knox Press, 2005).

15. Amos N. Wilder, "The Rhetoric of Ancient and Modern Apocalyptic," *Interpretation* 25, no. 4 (October 1971): 437 and 440, respectively.

16. Arthur Porritt, *John Henry Jowett* (London: Hodder & Stoughton, 1924), 299. For an excellent treatment of Jowett's preaching, and the preparation that preceded it, see *Twenty Centuries of Great Preaching: An Encyclopedia of Preaching*, ed. Clyde E. Fant Jr. and William M. Pinson Jr. (Waco, TX: Word Books, 1971), esp. 8:51–60.

17. See Arthur J. Gossip, *In Christ's Stead: The Warrack Lectures for 1925* (Grand Rapids: Baker Book House, 1968), 90.

18. Gardner C. Taylor, *How Shall They Preach* (Elgin, IL: Progressive Baptist Publishing House, 1977), 59.

19. Ibid., 60.

20. E. David Willis, "Rhetoric and Responsibility in Calvin's Theology," in *The Context of Contemporary Theology: Essays in Honor of Paul Lehmann*, ed. Alexander J. McKelway and E. David Willis (Atlanta: John Knox Press, 1974), 43–63. See also Quirinus Breen, "John Calvin and the Rhetorical Tradition," *Church History* 26 (1957): 3–21.

21. See Wesley's *Explanatory Notes upon the New Testament* (London: Epworth Press, 1952), preface.

22. See Wesley's "Directions Concerning Pronunciation and Gestures," in *The Works of The Rev. John Wesley, A.M.*, ed. John Emory (New York: J. Emory & B. Waugh, 1831), 487–93. See also W. L. Doughty, *John Wesley: Preacher* (London: Epworth Press, 1955), esp. 139–59.

23. Morgan Phelps Noyes, *Preaching the Word of God* (New York: Charles Scribner's Sons, 1943), 7.

24. Gossip, *In Christ's Stead*, 25.

25. T. Harwood Pattison, The *History of Christian Preaching* (Philadelphia: American Baptist Publication Society, 1903), statement on title page.

Chapter 4: The Steward and Ritual

1. Russell Brain, *The Nature of Experience* (London: Oxford University Press, 1959), 46.

2. Miles Mark Fisher, *Negro Slave Songs in the United States* (New York: Citadel Press, 1953), 33–35.

3. Ibid., 34.

4. On the concept of Holy Book, see *Holy Book and Holy Tradition*, ed. F. F. Bruce and E. G. Rupp (Grand Rapids: Wm. B. Eerdmans Pub. Co., 1968), esp. 1–19.

5. On the ritualistic import of space, see Patrick J. Quinn, "Ritual and the Definition of Space," in *The Roots of Ritual*, ed. James D. Shaughnessy (Grand Rapids: Wm. B. Eerdmans Pub. Co., 1973), 103–19.

6. Ibid., 104.

7. Paul W. Pruyser, *A Dynamic Psychology of Religion* (New York and Evanston: Harper & Row, 1968), 31.

8. See Stephen G. Meyer, "Neuropsychology and Worship," *Journal of Psychology and Theology* vol. 3, no. 4 (Fall 1975): 281–89.

9. Phillips Brooks, *Lectures on Preaching* (New York: E. P. Dutton & Co., 1877), 5.

10. On this combination of mediated meaning and mediated Presence, see James Earl Massey, *The Sermon in Perspective: A Study in Communication and Charisma* (Grand Rapids: Baker Book House, and Anderson, IN: Warner Press, 1976), esp. 105–13.

11. See Douglas Horton, *The Meaning of Worship: The Lyman Beecher Lectures for 1958* (New York: Harper & Bros., 1959), esp. 26–29.

12. Ibid., 75.

13. Margaret Mead, "Ritual and Social Crisis," in *The Roots of Ritual*, ed. James D. Shaughnessy, esp. 87–88.

14. See J. L. Austin, *Philosophical Papers* (Oxford: Clarendon Press, 1961),

chap. 9. See also a discussion of Austin's illustration in Bernard Mayo's article "The Moral Agent," in *The Human Agent: Royal Institute of Philosophy Lectures* (New York: St. Martin's Press, 1968), esp. 1:58–62.

15. Cited by Thomas E. Clarke, SJ, *New Pentecost or New Passion? The Direction of Religious Life Today* (New York and Toronto: Paulist Press, 1973), see 58–59.

16. See T. W. Manson, *The Teaching of Jesus: Studies in Its Form and Content* (Cambridge: Cambridge University Press, 1967), 207–9; Joachim Jeremias, *The Prayers of Jesus*, Studies in Biblical Theology, Second Series, no. 6 (London: SCM Press, 1967), 112–15.

17. Gerald S. Strober, *Graham: A Day in Billy's Life* (Garden City, NY: Doubleday & Co., 1976), 39. See also John Pollock, *Billy Graham: The Authorized Biography* (New York: McGraw-Hill Book Co., 1966), 53, 125, and *Just as I Am: The Autobiography of Billy Graham* (San Francisco: HarperSanFrancisco, 1997).

18. David H. C. Read, *Sent from God: The Enduring Power and Mystery of Preaching*, 1973 Lyman Beecher Lectures on Preaching (Nashville: Abingdon Press, 1974), 56.

Chapter 5: The Steward and Reality

1. John Kelman, *The War and Preaching* (New Haven, CT: Yale University Press, 1919), esp. 1–22.

2. Ibid., 6.

3. See Wade Robinson, *The Philosophy of the Atonement and Other Sermons* (London: J. M. Dent & Sons, 1912), esp. 1, 3.

4. Willard L. Sperry, *Reality in Worship: A Study of Public Worship and Private Devotion* (New York: Macmillan Co., 1927), 206.

5. On the subject of the religious in experience, see John Dewey, *A Common Faith* (New Haven, CT: Yale University Press, 1960 edition), esp. 22ff. Dewey's study on this subject is illuminating despite his own religious orientation as a humanistic naturalist.

6. Helmut Thielicke, *The Evangelical Faith*, trans. Geoffrey W. Bromiley (Grand Rapids: Wm. B. Eerdmans Pub. Co., 1974), 1:196.

7. Samuel H. Miller, *The Dilemma of Modern Belief: The Lyman Beecher Lectures 1972* (New York: Harper & Row, 1973), x.

8. See *Some Living Masters of the Pulpit: Studies in Religious Personality* (New York: George H. Doran Co., 1923), vii.

9. See Willard Brewing, "The Sermon I Might Have Preached, If!" in *Here Is My Method: The Art of Sermon Construction*, ed. Donald Macleod (Westwood, NJ: Fleming H. Revell, 1952), 37.

10. See Harry C. Howard, *Princes of the Christian Pulpit and Pastorate* (Nashville: Cokesbury Press, 1928), 238.

11. See Ridgely Torrence, *The Story of John Hope* (New York: Macmillan Co., 1948), 328.

12. The grammatical difficulties in the Greek text do not allow one to settle the argument about how the criticism should be viewed. The diatribe

word *phesin* could be a supposed objector or a real one. See F. Blass, A. Debrunner, R. W. Funk, *A Greek Grammar of the New Testament* (Chicago: University of Chicago Press, 1961), sections 130:3; 145:2. See also Ralph P. Martin, *2 Corinthians*, Word Biblical Commentary (Waco, TX: Word Books, 1986), 311–13; Victor Paul Furnish, *II Corinthians: Translated with Introduction, Notes, and Commentary*, Anchor Bible (Garden City, NY: Doubleday & Co., 1984), esp. 468–69, 478–79.

13. Cited by Alexander Gammie, *Preachers I Have Heard* (London: Pickering & Inglis, n.d.), 25.

14. Ibid., 61.

15. Cited by Howard, *Princes of the Christian Pulpit and Pastorate*, 280.

16. See A. W. W. Dale, *The Life of R. W. Dale of Birmingham* (London: Hodder & Stoughton, 1898), 132, 148; for Dale's earlier bouts with depression, see 60, 79–80, 115–17.

17. Stopford Brooke, *Life and Letters of Frederick W. Robertson* (London: Kegan Paul, Trench, Truebner & Co., 1891), 2:223; James R. Blackwood, *The Soul of Frederick W. Robertson: The Brighton Preacher* (New York: Harper & Bros., 1947), esp. 167–80, which treat the circumstances of Robertson's physical suffering and death.

18. John Hall, *His Word through Preaching* (New York: Dodd & Mead, 1875), 82.

19. See W. Robertson Nicoll, *Princes of the Church* (London: Hodder & Stoughton, 1921), 278.

20. From "Something Left Undone," in *The Complete Poetical Works of Henry Wadsworth Longfellow* (Boston and New York: Houghton & Mifflin Co., 1893), 203.

21. See Taylor Branch, *Parting the Waters: America in the King Years, 1954–1963* (New York: Simon & Schuster, 1988), 902.

22. Samuel D. Proctor, *My Moral Odyssey* (Valley Forge, PA: Judson Press, 1989), 176.

23. Charles Wesley, from his hymn "A Charge to Keep I Have."

Chapter 6: The Gracious Imperative

1. From "Andrew," by Clive Sansom, in *The Witnesses* (London: David Higham Associates, 1956), 13–14.

2. David S. Bell, "A Fishing Story," in *Best Sermons* 7, ed. James W. Cox and Kenneth M. Cox (New York: HarperCollins Publishers, 1994), 19–20.

3. See *The Mishnah*, trans. Herbert Danby (London: Oxford University Press, 1933), Berakoth 2:2, p. 3.

4. On some deutero-canonical parallels to the invitational wording in Matthew 11:29a, see Ecclesiasticus 24:19–22 and 51:23–27.

5. On this as a comprehensive metaphor, see Wilhelm H. Wuellner, *The Meaning of "Fishers of Men"* (Philadelphia: Westminster Press, 1967), esp. 134–231.

6. "We Will Work for Jesus," Hymn 257 in *Hymnal of the Church of God* (Anderson, IN: Warner Press, 1971).

Chapter 7: On Being a Leader

1. Ralph Waldo Emerson, *Essays and Lectures*, ed. and comp. Joel Porte (New York: Library of America, 1983), 971.
2. *The Works of Aristotle*, vol. 2 (Chicago: Encyclopaedia Britannica, 1952), bk. 7. chap. 14, p. 537.

Chapter 8: This Jesus

1. *Contemporary Thinking about Jesus: An Anthology* (Nashville: Abingdon-Cokesbury Press, 1944), 7.
2. On this see Emil Schurer, *The History of the Jewish People in the Age of Jesus Christ (175 B.C.–A.D. 135)*, new English version rev. and ed. Geza Vermes and Fergus Millar (Edinburgh: T. & T. Clark, 1973), 1:431.
3. Cited from *Münchener Katholische Kirchenzeitung* 35 (1946): 27f.
4. See the discussion by Don Alois Mager, "Satan in Our Day," in *Satan*, trans. from *Etudes Carmelitaines*, ed. Pere Bruno de Jesus-Maria (New York: Sheed & Ward, 1952), 501.
5. Cited by Mager, "Satan in Our Day," 503.
6. James Moffatt, *A Critical and Exegetical Commentary on the Epistle to the Hebrews* (Edinburgh: T. & T. Clark, 1952), 6.
7. Daniel T. Niles, *Upon the Earth* (Boston: McGraw-Hill Book Co., 1963), 63.
8. On this, see Peter T. O'Brien, *The Epistle to the Philippians: A Commentary on the Greek Text*, New International Greek Testament Commentary (Grand Rapids: Wm. B. Eerdmans Pub. Co., 1991), esp. 237–42.

Chapter 9: On Being Responsible

1. See Thomas Mann, *Joseph in Egypt*, trans. H. T. Lowe-Porter (New York: Alfred A. Knopf, 1938), esp. 2:370–71.
2. See Flavius Josephus, *Antiquities of the Jews*, bk. 2, chap. 9, par. 7.
3. See Søren Kierkegaard, *The Last Years*, ed. and trans. Ronald Gregor Smith (New York: Harper & Row, 1965), 133.

Chapter 10: Stay in the Race!

1. See E. Norman Gardiner, *Athletes of the Ancient World* (Oxford: Clarendon Press, 1955), 58.
2. Xenophon, *Memorabilia and Oeconomicus*, trans. E. C. Marchant, Loeb Classical Library (Cambridge, MA: Harvard University Press, 1953), see 249–53.
3. On these spirituals, see John Lovell Jr., *Black Song: The Forge and the Flame* (New York: Paragon House Publishers, 1972), esp. 322–23, 379.
4. Benjamin E. Mays, *Lord, the People Have Driven Me On* (New York and Atlanta: Vantage Press, 1981), 4.

Chapter 11: When Devotion Meets Difficulty

1. John Locke, *Some Thoughts concerning Education*, par. 127, as reprinted in *John Locke on Education*, ed. Peter Gay (New York: Teachers College, Columbia University, 1964), 93.

2. Samuel DeWitt Proctor, *The Substance of Things Hoped For: A Memoir of African-American Faith* (New York: G. P. Putnam's Sons, 1995), 81–83.

3. "Slav'ry Chain," as sung by Catherine Fields-Gay, from the collection by R. Nathaniel Dett. See his *Religious Folk-Songs of the Negro as Sung at Hampton Institute* (Hampton, VA: Hampton Institute Press, 1927), 112.

Index of Names

Achtemeier, Elizabeth, 16
Aristotle, 64
Augustine, Aurelius (St.), 7-8, 33
Austin, J. L., 39

Bailey, E. K., xvi
Barber, George, 47
Beare, Francis Wright, 21
Beecher Lectures, 23, 33, 47, 48, 49
Beeson Divinity School, xi, xvi
Bell, David S., 52
Born to Rebel (Mays), 82
Brain, Russell, 36
Brewing, Willard, 45
Brooks, Phillips, 23, 38
Brown, Ronald, 86
Brueggemann, Walter, 13
Buber, Martin, 22

Calvin, John, 33
Carver, George Washington, 4
Christian Brotherhood Hour, ix
Church of God (Anderson, IN), ix
Conger Lectures, xi, xvi

Contemporary Thinking about Jesus (Kepler), 67
Cooper, Imogen, 12
Cornerstone Baptist Church, 50
Corts, Thomas E., xvi
Culpepper, R. Alan, xvi
Cummings, Charles, 90

Dale, R. W., 47-48
Designing the Sermon, 17
Dexter Avenue Baptist Church, 49

Elizabeth, Queen of England, 74
Emerson, Ralph Waldo, 20, 63

Fisher, Miles Mark, 36

George, Timothy, xvi
God Who Acts (Wright), 13
Gossip, Arthur John, 32, 34
Graham, Billy, 40

Haile Selassie I, Emperor, 74
Haley, Alex, 14

Hall, John, 48
Harvard Divinity School, ix
Herbert, George, xiii
Hitler, Adolf, 69
Hope, John, 45
Horne, Charles Sylvester, 49
Horton, Douglas, 38
Hoskyns, Edwyn C., xii
Howard, Harry C., 45
Howard University, xvi, 49

James, John Angell, 48
Johns, Vernon, 49
Josephus, Flavius, 68, 75
Jowett, John Henry, 32

Kafka, Franz, 39
Kelman, John, 41
Kennedy, President John F., 86
Kepler, Thomas S., 67
Kierkegaard, Sᵉren, 76
King, Martin Luther, Jr., 49, 86

Ladd, George Eldon, 22
Lindblom, J., 27
Locke, John, 87
Longfellow, Henry Wadsworth, 49
Luther, Martin, 20

MacDonald, George, xiii
Macgregor, James, 47
Mann, Thomas, 73
Marcel, Gabriel, 3
Mays, Benjamin E., 82
McAfee School of Theology, xvi
Mead, Margaret, 39
Mercer University, xvi
Miller, Samuel H., 44
Morehouse College, 45
Morison, James, 47
Morris, Leon, 21

Newton, Joseph Fort, 44
Nicoll, W. Robertson, 49
Niles, Daniel T., 70
Noyes, Morgan Phelps, 34

Old Testament and the Proclamation
    of the Gospel, The (Achtemeier), 16
On Christian Doctrine (Augustine), 8
On Teaching the Uninitiated (Augustine), 8

Pattison, T. Harwood, 34
Phillips School of Theology, xvi
Politics (Aristotle), 64
Proctor, Samuel DeWitt, 50,
    88-89
Pruyser, Paul W., 38

Quinn, Paul J., 37

Rankin Chapel, xvi
Ray, Sandy F., 49-50
Read, David H. C., 40
Robertson, Frederick William, 48
Robinson, Wade, 42

Samford University, xvi
Sanders, James A., 15
Sansom, Clive, 52
Schultz, Charles, 7
Self Lectures, xvi
Socrates, 78
Sperry, Willard L., 43
spirituals, 36, 78-80, 90
Stott, John, 21

Taylor, Gardner C., 5, 22, 32
Taylor, Laura, 5
Taylor, Vincent, 21
Thielicke, Helmut, 43
Tuskegee Institute, 25

Virginia Union University, 88-89
von Rad, Gerhard, 12

Warner, Daniel S., 57
Warrack Lectures, 32
Washington, Booker T., 25
Wesley, John, 33-34
Wesleyan Quadrilateral Method, 2

Wilder, Amos N., 16, 31
Willis, E. David, 33
Wittgenstein, Ludwig, 18
Wright, G. Ernest, 13

Xenophon, 78

Yale Divinity School, 23, 41

Index of Biblical References

Old Testament

Genesis
1:1	19
15:2	1
24:1-67	1
43:19-24	1
44:1-6	1

Psalm
18:30	62-63
29:2	36
42:7	32

Proverbs
14:12	69
18:16	46

Isaiah
55:1-7	59-60
55:10-11	27

Jeremiah
10:1	27

Ezekiel
45:9	27

Amos
3:8b	27

New Testament

Matthew
5:16	xii
6:22	38
11:29a	54
13:54-56	70
20:8-9	2
24:14	22
25:21	50

Mark
1:16-20	51
3:14-15	70
4:34a	18
6:30	70
12:37	18
16:1-6	85

Luke
2:1-7	70
3:23	70
8:38-39	56

11:34	38
12:42-43	10
16:1-8	2
23:13-25	71

John
4:35	57
13:34-35	xii
20:31	14
21:17	57
21:19b	55

Acts
2:36	64
4:12	71
8:30-31	32
20:27	22

Romans
2:25	21
3:24	21
4:25	91
5:9	21
5:10	21
6:3-7	21
10:8-10	22

Romans (*continued*)
10:14-15a 37
10:17 15
15:4 14, 28

1 Corinthians
1:21 37
1:23 21
2:1-2 20
4:1-2 2, 6
9:16-17 6
11:1 65
12:4-6 46
13:9a 49
14:7 38

2 Corinthians
3:2-3 x
4:5 22
4:7-10 45-46
10:10 47
11:24-25 47

Galatians
3:1 20
5:24 21
6:14 21

Ephesians
1:3-14 30
1:15-23 30
2:1-7 30

2:11-12 30
2:14-16 30
2:19-22 30
3:1-7 30
3:8-12 30
3:9 21
3:14-19 30
4:1-6 30
4:11-16 30
4:17-19 30
4:20-24 30
4:21 20
5:3-5 30
5:18-23 30
5:25-27 30
5:28-30 30
6:1-3 30
6:5-8 30
6:14-24 30

Philippians
2:6-11 5
2:9-11 71

Colossians
2:11-13 21

1 Timothy
1:15 xiii
2:6 21
3:16 5

2 Timothy
2:15 8
4:2 9

Titus
1:7 2

Hebrews
1:1 xii
1:3 69
1:6b 69-70
1:8a 70
1:10 70
1:12b 70
7:16 71
7:25 71
11:6b 42
11:24-26 73
12:1-2 77
13:8 67
13:9a 72
13:15 72

1 Peter
2:21-24a 65
4:10 2

Revelation
2:10b 50
21:1 15